STRAIT OF TENSIONS

GEW REPORTS &
ANALYSES TEAM

STRAIT OF TENSIONS

THE GEOPOLITICAL TURMOIL OF BAB EL-MANDEB

Global East-West (London)

CONTENTS

CONTENTS

MAP: STRAIT OF TENSION

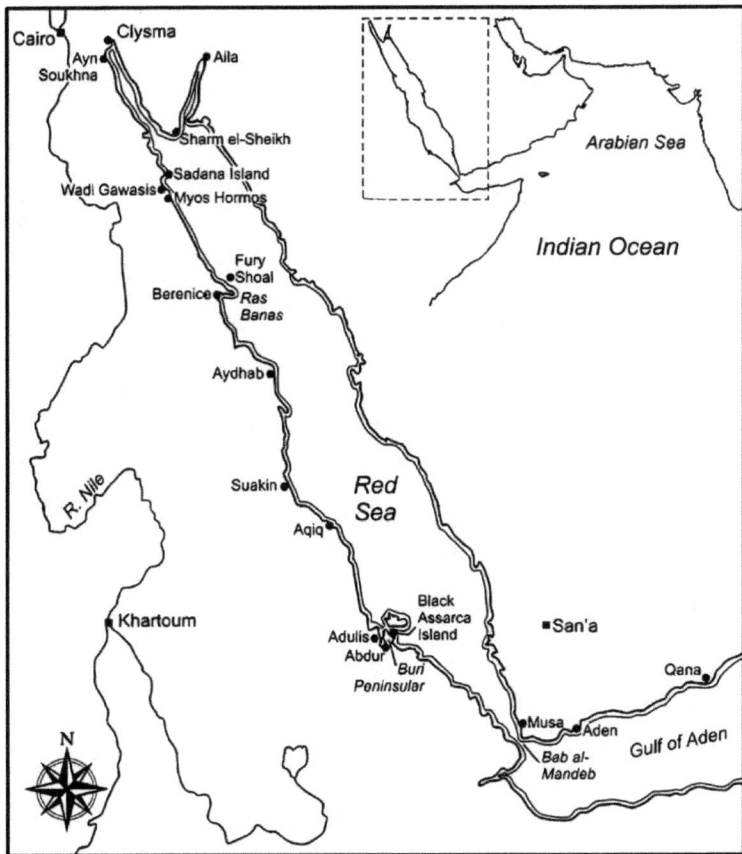

Strait of Tensions
GEW

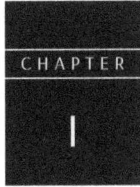

INTRODUCTION

The Red Sea is a body of water steeped in rich history and strategic importance. Its significance as a key maritime route connecting the Mediterranean Sea to the Indian Ocean cannot be overstated, making any disturbances in this region a cause for global concern.

For centuries, the Red Sea has served as a vital trade route, facilitating the exchange of goods, ideas, and cultures between nations. Merchants and explorers traversed its waters, navigating through its narrow straits and encountering a diverse array of civilizations along the way. Even today, this historic trade route remains of utmost importance, serving as a gateway for international commerce, particularly for energy resources such as oil and gas.

In recent years, the Red Sea has experienced an alarming increase in attacks on commercial ships, raising significant concerns about maritime trade stability in the region. A multitude of factors contribute to these growing risks. Geopolitical tensions, piracy threats, and conflicts in nearby regions have created a volatile environment, jeopardizing the safety of vessels navigating these waters.

One of the key chokepoints in the Red Sea is the Bab el Mandeb strait, a narrow waterway situated between the coasts of Yemen and the African continent. This strait holds immense strategic and economic significance, acting as a doorway to the Suez Canal and ultimately, the Mediterranean Sea. Any disturbances to the safe passage of ships through the Bab el Mandeb can have far-reaching consequences for global trade and the stability of the wider region.

The crisis in the Red Sea extends beyond a mere issue of maritime security; it has a direct impact on the cost of oil, which in turn affects economies across the globe. Given the region's importance as a major route for oil exports, any disruptions to the flow of oil through the Red Sea can have severe ramifications for global oil markets. Shipping delays, heightened risk of attacks, and potential blockades can lead to a sharp rise in oil prices, impacting industries and consumer prices worldwide.

Moreover, the Red Sea plays a vital role in the transportation of various other commodities, including but not limited to liquefied natural gas, agricultural products, and manufactured goods. The potential for shipping delays, higher transportation costs, and a slowdown in international trade due to the crisis further compounds the adverse impact on the global economy. Companies involved in maritime trade are compelled to reassess their routes, enhance security measures, and incur additional operational costs to mitigate risk, ultimately affecting profit margins and operational efficiency.

It is crucial to recognize that the crisis in the Red Sea is not an isolated incident but a reflection of wider geopolitical complexities. The region is characterized by deep-rooted tensions, long-standing conflicts, and international power struggles. Civil wars, territorial disputes, and power vacuums provide fertile ground for proxy wars and foreign interventions. Major global powers such as the United States, Russia, Iran, and Saudi Arabia have vested interests in the region, further exacerbating the complex dynamics at play.

The strategic importance of chokepoints in the Red Sea cannot be understated, with the Suez Canal and the Bab el Mandeb serving as gateways for global maritime trade. Controlling these chokepoints provides immense influence over international politics and power dynamics. As a result, interstate rivalry and competition among regional powers, including Iran, Saudi Arabia, Egypt, and their respective allies, intensify the crisis. As each seeks to secure its interests, the risks and threats to marine safety and stability in the Red Sea region only continue to grow.

Furthermore, the crisis is compounded by ethnic and religious divides within the region. Ongoing conflicts in Yemen, Sudan, and Eritrea have heightened tensions and fueled instability. Sectarian strife between Sunni and Shia Muslims further hampers diplomatic efforts to resolve the crisis, hindering the path toward stability. Notably, external powers have been known to form alliances based on religious principles, further adding complexity to an already intricate situation.

Addressing the crisis in the Red Sea requires a comprehensive approach that tackles the immediate security concerns while addressing the underlying political, economic, and social factors. International cooperation plays a pivotal role in this regard. Countries with vested interests in the region, such as the United States, European nations, and Gulf states, must engage in constructive diplomatic efforts to reduce tensions and find peaceful solutions to the conflicts fueling the crisis.

Moreover, enhancing maritime security in the Red Sea is crucial to protect commercial shipping. Collaborative efforts form an essential part of ensuring the safety of vessels. These efforts can include the deployment of naval forces, the establishment of international patrols, and increased intelligence sharing to counter piracy and other security threats. Supporting regional initiatives and organizations that promote stability in the Red Sea region is also vital, including efforts to strengthen governance and address economic disparities.

In conclusion, the crisis unfolding in the Red Sea

poses a serious risk to international trade stability and global economic prosperity. It demands a comprehensive and multifaceted approach that addresses the underlying geopolitical complexities, supports regional stability, and enhances maritime security. Immediate global cooperation is imperative, recognizing the interconnectedness of various factors contributing to the crisis. It is through a concerted effort that long-term solutions can be achieved to ensure stability in the Red Sea region, protect vital trade routes, and safeguard the global economy as a whole.

A. OVERVIEW OF THE RECENT UPTICK IN ATTACKS ON COMMERCIAL SHIPS IN THE RED SEA

In recent years, the Red Sea has experienced a disturbing surge in attacks on commercial ships, causing widespread concern for global trade and maritime security. This chapter provides an in-depth analysis of this concerning trend, exploring its origins, causes, and far-reaching consequences.

The Red Sea holds immense strategic importance as a crucial maritime route connecting the Mediterranean

Sea to the Indian Ocean. Ships passing through this vital pathway facilitate the transportation of goods, including oil, between regions. However, the alarming rise in attacks on commercial ships in this region has not only disrupted the smooth flow of goods but has also posed a significant threat to the safety of seafarers.

Geopolitical tensions and ongoing regional conflicts have served as catalysts for these attacks. The Red Sea region is plagued by territorial disputes, heightening rivalries, and long-standing conflicts such as the Yemeni civil war and the tensions between Iran and Saudi Arabia. These tensions have created an unstable environment, ideal for piracy and other criminal activities. As various actors seek to assert their influence or further their political and economic agendas, commercial ships have become targets in this volatile theatre.

One key flashpoint in the region is the Bab el Mandeb strait, situated at the southern end of the Red Sea. This strategic chokepoint acts as a gateway to the Suez Canal, through which a significant portion of global trade, including oil shipments, transits. Controlling this strait holds immense value for various actors seeking to project power and gain geopolitical advantage. Consequently, the increased threats to commercial ships in the Red Sea are often connected to rivalries over control of this critical maritime chokepoint.

The vulnerabilities of global energy supply chains to disruptions in the Red Sea have raised serious concerns. Major oil-producing countries, such as Saudi Arabia, rely heavily on the Red Sea for the transportation of their oil exports. Disruptions in shipping routes due to attacks on commercial ships not only hamper these countries' ability to export oil but can also lead to reduced oil supply globally. Such disruptions can trigger sharp increases in oil prices on the international market, potentially impacting economies worldwide.

Additionally, the geographic proximity of the Red Sea to conflict-ridden areas such as the Horn of Africa further exacerbates the security challenges faced in the region. Somalia, for example, has been a hotbed for maritime piracy in recent years. The presence of these criminal networks and their ability to launch attacks on commercial ships in the Red Sea adds another layer of complexity. The nefarious activities of pirates, terrorists, and other organized criminal groups have contributed to the rise in attacks and insecurity in the region.

The implications of maritime security concerns in the Red Sea extend beyond oil. The region serves as a crucial artery for the transportation of various commodities, including minerals, agricultural goods, and manufactured products. Delays in shipping, higher transportation costs, and a slowdown in international trade are all potential consequences of the instability caused by attacks on commercial ships in the Red Sea area.

Moreover, the safety and well-being of seafarers are at stake in the face of these attacks. These individuals, often working in challenging conditions, are subjected to significant risks when navigating through the Red Sea.

Attacks on ships, including hijackings, armed robberies, and kidnappings, not only threaten their lives but also impact their mental and physical well-being. The lasting traumatic effects of these incidents on seafarers and their families cannot be overstated.

The crisis in the Red Sea has compelled maritime companies to reassess their routes and enhance their security protocols, resulting in increased operational costs. Recognizing the critical importance of safeguarding their personnel and assets, these companies have adopted comprehensive security measures to mitigate the risks posed by piracy and attacks.

To navigate this increasingly complex security landscape, international cooperation is paramount. Collaborative efforts between regional and international actors are vital to monitor, deter, and respond effectively to the threats faced by commercial ships in the Red Sea. The establishment of multinational naval task forces and the sharing of intelligence and information can enhance the overall security of the region, deterring potential attackers and mitigating the risks associated with piracy.

In conclusion, the recent escalation in attacks on commercial ships in the Red Sea presents significant challenges to global trade and maritime security. The interplay of geopolitical tensions, regional conflicts, the strategic significance of the Red Sea, and the presence of organized criminal groups contribute to this crisis. Addressing these challenges requires a concerted effort from the international community to ensure stability in the Red Sea region and protect the global economy from the adverse impacts of maritime insecurity. Safeguarding the lives and well-being of seafarers, enhancing security measures, and promoting global cooperation are essential elements in the efforts to counter these threats and preserve the integrity of the Red Sea as a crucial maritime route.

B. IMPORTANCE OF THE RED SEA AS A VITAL MARITIME ROUTE LINKING THE MEDITERRANEAN SEA TO THE INDIAN OCEAN

The Red Sea, a body of water located between the Arabian Peninsula and Northeast Africa, has captured the imagination of explorers, traders, and nations for centuries. It is a veritable tapestry of history, culture, and geopolitics, serving as a conduit for exchange between diverse civilizations.

Ancient civilizations recognized the strategic importance of the Red Sea, utilizing its waters to expand their influence and trade networks. The Pharaohs of ancient Egypt employed the Red Sea as a gateway to the fabled

Land of Punt, a source of exotic goods such as gold, incense, ebony, and ivory. This maritime link enabled the Egyptians to establish diplomatic ties, acquire valuable resources, and enhance their cultural wealth.

In later centuries, the Phoenicians, renowned seafarers and traders, capitalized on the Red Sea's position to forge lucrative connections with the civilizations of the Indian subcontinent. These maritime pioneers established colonies, such as Aden and Socotra, which facilitated the exchange of goods and ideas, as well as cultural and religious diffusion.

Greek exploration and colonization in the Red Sea region further shaped its historical trajectory. Led by mariners like Eudoxus of Cyzicus and Hippalus, Greek merchants ventured beyond the known Mediterranean world, discovering new trade routes to the Arabian Peninsula and East Africa. These explorations laid the foundation for the vibrant commercial networks that emerged during the Hellenistic and Roman eras.

Beyond its role as a hub of commerce and cultural exchange, the Red Sea witnessed the rise of Islam and the rapid expansion of Muslim empires. The Prophet Muhammad's migration from Mecca to Medina, known as the Hijra, took place along the northern Arabian coast of the Red Sea. This event marked a profound shift in the balance of power and heralded the birth of a new civilization. The Red Sea became an integral part of the emerging Islamic civilization, serving as a maritime lifeline for the spread of Islam and the establishment of vibrant trade networks.

During the Islamic Golden Age, the Red Sea's significance as a trade route intensified. Arab traders, well-versed in navigation and maritime activities, facilitated the exchange of goods, ideas, and scientific knowledge between the Islamic world, India, China, and the Mediterranean. The legendary city of Jeddah became a bustling entrepôt, attracting merchants from around the world. It served as a gateway to the Muslim world, providing access to the sacred cities of Mecca and Medina.

The Red Sea's importance extended well beyond religious and cultural spheres. Its waters were a vital link in the chain of global trade during the medieval period. Arab traders carried coveted goods like silk, porcelain, and spices from distant lands, establishing connections between Europe, Asia, and Africa. This booming trade not only enriched the merchants but also fostered intellectual, artistic, and technological exchanges. The maritime cities of Aden, Berenice, and Suez thrived as centers of commerce and cross-cultural encounters, epitomizing the Red Sea's dynamic nature.

With the dawn of the modern era, the Red Sea's role as a global trading route underwent significant transformations. The opening of the Suez Canal in 1869 further enhanced its importance, enabling efficient connectivity between the Mediterranean and the Indian Ocean. This engineering marvel revolutionized maritime trade, reducing travel times and facilitating the movement of goods, people, and ideas.

As the 20th century unfolded, the Red Sea's strategic significance gained geopolitical dimensions. The emergence of oil-rich nations on its shores, such as Saudi Arabia and Yemen, added new layers of complexity to regional dynamics. The Red Sea's crucial shipping route became indispensable for the transportation of oil and gas resources to global markets. Maintaining the security and safety of this vital maritime corridor became vital for these nations and, indeed, for the uninterrupted flow of energy to the world.

The Red Sea's location adjacent to emerging economic powerhouses, particularly China and India, propelled its strategic value even further. It is an essential gateway for these nations to access the markets of Europe, Africa, and the Middle East. The Red Sea's deep-water ports, with their modern infrastructure and logistical capabilities, attract investment and aid in the development of vibrant economic zones.

However, the Red Sea's prosperity also faces challenges. The delicate marine ecosystems, including coral reefs and mangrove forests, are under immense pressure due to pollution, climate change, and overfishing. International efforts for marine conservation and sustainable development are critical to protect these fragile and diverse ecosystems.

The Red Sea's geopolitics are equally complex. The waterway has become a focal point for regional rivalries and conflicts. Yemen's ongoing civil war, for example, threatens the stability of the Bab el-Mandeb Strait, a narrow passage connecting the Red Sea to the Gulf of Aden. The presence of international powers, such as the United States, China, and Russia, seeking to safeguard their interests, adds further layers of complexity to the region's geopolitical landscape.

In conclusion, the Red Sea's journey through time has intertwined with the destinies of nations, shaped trade networks, and showcased the dynamism of human interaction. From ancient civilizations to the modern age, its strategic significance has only increased, with economic, cultural, and geopolitical dimensions converging in this vital waterway. Preserving its environmental integrity and managing its complex geopolitical dynamics require international cooperation and a long-term vision to ensure the continued prosperity and sustainability of the Red Sea for future generations.

C. THESIS STATEMENT: ANALYZING THE ORIGINS, EFFECTS ON OIL PRICES, AND WIDER CONSEQUENCES FOR GLOBAL TRADE

The Red Sea crisis has emerged as a pressing issue in recent years, with a surge in attacks on commercial ships. This chapter delves into the origins of these attacks, examining the underlying geopolitical tensions, piracy, and regional conflicts that have contributed to this alarming trend.

The Red Sea, located between Africa and Asia, is a critical maritime route linking the Mediterranean Sea to the Indian Ocean. Its strategic importance as a major trade corridor has made it a focal point for various actors seeking to assert control over this vital waterway. This contention has been further exacerbated by long-standing political and sectarian rivalries in the region.

One of the key drivers of the increased attacks in the Red Sea is piracy, which has plagued the area for centuries. Piracy is rooted in socio-economic factors, such as poverty, unemployment, and a lack of alternative livelihoods for coastal communities. In Somalia, for example, poverty and lawlessness have provided fertile ground for pirate groups to operate, with the promise of lucrative ransom payments from hijacked vessels. Furthermore, the limited capacity of regional navies to effectively patrol vast maritime areas has allowed pirate networks to thrive. The lack of central governance in Somalia and unsuccessful attempts to establish a functioning government have created a vacuum in law enforcement, allowing piracy to persist.

Additionally, the instability in nearby countries, such

as Yemen, has created a breeding ground for piracy, allowing criminal networks to flourish due to weak governance and limited law enforcement capabilities. The ongoing conflict in Yemen has significantly contributed to the escalation of maritime attacks. Houthi rebels, who control key parts of Yemen's Red Sea coastline, have actively targeted ships passing through the region, using both conventional weapons and asymmetric tactics. This not only poses a direct threat to maritime security but also exacerbates tensions between regional actors, such as Saudi Arabia and Iran, who support opposing sides in the conflict.

Complicating matters further, the Red Sea has become a battleground for regional conflicts and power struggles. The rivalry between Saudi Arabia and Iran, commonly referred to as the "Cold War of the Middle East," has intensified in recent years, with the Red Sea becoming a critical theater of this competition. Iran has sought to expand its influence by supporting proxy groups, such as the Houthi rebels in Yemen, while Saudi Arabia has formed alliances with countries such as Egypt and Jordan to counter these Iranian-backed forces. As a result, the Red Sea has become an arena where geopolitical tensions are played out, increasing the risk of maritime attacks.

The surge in attacks on commercial ships in the Red Sea has had broader implications for global energy markets. Given the region's proximity to major oil-producing countries like Saudi Arabia and the United

Arab Emirates, any disruptions to shipping could significantly impact global oil prices. The threat of attacks has led to increased insurance costs for shipping companies, which, in turn, are passed onto consumers. Moreover, concerns over the safety of shipping routes have resulted in increased naval patrols and the deployment of private security contractors, further adding to transportation costs.

In addition to the direct impact on oil prices, the Red Sea crisis has wider consequences for global trade stability. Shipping delays and increased transportation costs translate into higher prices for goods, affecting both producers and consumers. For nations heavily reliant on trade, particularly those that rely on the Red Sea for imports and exports, these disruptions can have far-reaching economic ramifications. Additionally, the uncertainty surrounding maritime security in the Red Sea may lead to a reevaluation of global trade routes, potentially redirecting shipping traffic to longer and costlier alternatives.

Addressing the Red Sea crisis requires a multi-faceted approach involving regional cooperation, robust legal frameworks, and strengthened law enforcement capabilities. Enhancing maritime security through increased patrols, intelligence sharing, and capacity-building initiatives for coastal states is paramount. Combating piracy demands targeted efforts focused on addressing socio-economic issues, such as poverty and unemployment, as well as improving governance and law enforcement capacities in countries affected by piracy.

Furthermore, engaging with the regional actors involved in the conflicts that contribute to the Red Sea crisis is crucial. Diplomatic efforts to mitigate tensions, foster dialogue, and deescalate rivalries can help create a conducive environment for maritime security cooperation. International organizations, such as the United Nations and the African Union, can play critical roles in facilitating dialogue and supporting regional initiatives aimed at addressing the root causes of the crisis.

In conclusion, the Red Sea crisis represents a complex challenge that necessitates a comprehensive understanding of the underlying geopolitical tensions, piracy, and regional conflicts. By further exploring the socio-economic factors driving piracy, the regional conflicts exacerbating the crisis, and the implications for global trade stability, one can better comprehend the severity of the situation. Through addressing the root causes, strengthening maritime security, and fostering regional cooperation, the international community can work towards ensuring the safety and stability of this critical maritime corridor.

REVEALED: THE CRISIS AT THE RED SEA

The Red Sea has long played a crucial role in global trade, serving as a vital maritime route connecting the Mediterranean Sea to the Indian Ocean. In recent years, however, there has been a noticeable increase in attacks on commercial ships in this region, revealing a deepening crisis that threatens the stability of international trade.

The origins of this crisis can be traced back to a combination of geopolitical tensions, piracy, regional conflicts, and socio-economic challenges. Various states and non-state actors are vying for power and influence, leading to an environment of heightened insecurity. The region's strategic significance is further amplified by the Bab el

Mandeb strait, which serves as a gateway for maritime trade and is a critical chokepoint.

Geopolitically, the Red Sea region is a confluence of competing interests from major global powers. The United States, Russia, China, and European Union countries all seek to assert their influence and secure their economic and strategic objectives. The United States, although not a direct coastal state in the region, maintains a significant military presence and conducts regular naval exercises. Russia, on the other hand, has established military bases in Syria and has expanded its influence in the Eastern Mediterranean, projecting power into the Red Sea. China, with its Belt and Road Initiative, has shown growing interest in securing its maritime trade routes, including those passing through the Red Sea. European Union countries, particularly France and Italy, have deployed naval assets to protect their commercial interests and contribute to regional stability. This complex power play often exacerbates existing tensions and fuels proxy conflicts within the region.

One prominent driver of the crisis is the proliferation of piracy. While piracy has historically plagued these waters, its resurgence in recent years has further destabilized the region. Somali pirates, in particular, have posed a significant threat to maritime trade, with their attacks on commercial vessels and ransom demands causing disruptions and financial losses. Efforts to combat piracy have been partially successful, but the underlying factors driving this criminal activity, such as poverty and weak governance in Somalia, remain largely unaddressed.

The crisis in the Red Sea is not solely limited to piracy; it also encompasses broader regional conflicts. The ongoing conflict in Yemen, for instance, has spilled over into the maritime domain, with Houthi rebels targeting commercial ships transiting through the Bab el Mandeb strait. The Saudi-led coalition, supporting the Yemeni government, has conducted naval blockades and airstrikes in response, further escalating tensions in the region. This not only poses a direct threat to the safety of navigation but also exacerbates tensions between regional actors, particularly Saudi Arabia, Iran, and the United Arab Emirates.

Ethnic and religious complexities within the Red Sea region further contribute to the crisis. Tensions between Sunni and Shia communities, exemplified by the Saudi-Iran rivalry, add another layer of complexity to the maritime security challenge. State and non-state actors often exploit these fault lines, aggravating existing conflicts and impeding diplomatic efforts to find sustainable solutions.

Moreover, the crisis in the Red Sea region has significant implications for global energy security. The straits of Hormuz and Bab el Mandeb are vital routes for oil transportation, with nearly 10% of global oil trade passing through these chokepoints. Disruptions to shipping routes or attacks on tanker vessels could lead to a sharp increase in oil prices, affecting economies worldwide and compromising energy security.

The deepening crisis has prompted maritime companies and insurance agencies to reassess risk factors and security protocols. Increased costs for insurance premiums, vessel protection, and rerouting ships have resulted in elevated operational expenses, ultimately impacting consumers who bear the brunt of these additional costs. Moreover, the threat of attacks has led companies to develop innovative technologies and security measures to mitigate risks, such as the use of armed guards on ships, enhanced surveillance systems, and coordination with naval forces.

Addressing the crisis at the Red Sea requires a comprehensive and multi-faceted approach. Enhanced regional collaboration, intelligence sharing, and capacity-building initiatives are crucial to strengthen maritime security and counter piracy effectively. International organizations such as the United Nations and the International Maritime Organization should take an active role in facilitating dialogue and coordinating efforts among regional states, with the aim of harmonizing legal frameworks, sharing best practices, and establishing mechanisms for joint operations and information exchange. Simultaneously, efforts should be directed towards mitigating socio-economic challenges, promoting good governance, and fostering regional dialogue to resolve underlying conflicts.

The international community must play a more active

role in facilitating negotiations and seeking cooperative solutions to address the root causes of the crisis. Encouraging regional powers to engage in sustained diplomacy, promoting inclusive dialogue among conflicting parties, and supporting mechanisms for de-escalation are essential steps towards restoring stability and trade confidence in the Red Sea region. Alongside diplomatic initiatives, sustained investment in the development and capacity-building of coastal states, particularly Somalia and Yemen, will be crucial in addressing the economic and governance challenges that contribute to piracy and regional conflicts.

In summary, the revealed crisis in the Red Sea poses a serious risk to international trade stability and global security. The complex interplay of geopolitical rivalries, piracy, regional conflicts, and socio-economic challenges requires comprehensive and sustained international cooperation. By addressing the underlying causes and fostering dialogue among conflicting parties, the crisis can be effectively managed, ensuring the safety of maritime trade routes and safeguarding vital global interests.

A. HISTORICAL SIGNIFICANCE OF THE RED SEA IN GLOBAL TRADE

The Red Sea holds a significant place in the history of global trade. Stretching across 1,900 kilometers between Africa and Asia, it has served as a vital maritime route connecting the Mediterranean Sea to the Indian Ocean. The Red Sea's strategic location at the crossroads of major trade routes has facilitated the exchange of goods, ideas, and cultures for centuries, shaping the world we know today.

One of the earliest recorded uses of the Red Sea for trade dates back to ancient Egypt, one of the world's first great civilizations. The Pharaohs recognized the importance of the Red Sea as a trade route and established links with Arabia and East Africa. Egyptian fleets sailed across the Red Sea, not only to acquire valuable goods such as spices, incense, and exotic animals but also to establish diplomatic relations with neighboring kingdoms. The Red Sea's convenient location made it an ideal point of convergence for trade from Africa, Asia, and Europe.

The prosperity and influence of Red Sea trade reached its peak during the Hellenistic period. Under the Ptolemaic dynasty, which ruled Egypt from Alexandria, maritime trade expanded significantly. Egyptian rule extended further south, encompassing the coastal areas of modern-day Sudan and Eritrea. This expansion led to the establishment of prosperous port cities along the Red Sea coast, such as Berenice and Myos Hormos. These cities served as crucial gateway ports for goods that would eventually reach Rome and other parts of the Mediterranean.

Trade in the Red Sea during the Hellenistic period was not limited to goods. It also fostered cultural exchange and the spread of ideas. Greek, Egyptian, and Arabian influences intertwined along the shores of the Red Sea, leading to an amalgamation of traditions, languages, and customs. The exchange of knowledge and ideas between different civilizations contributed to the rich diversity of the region.

With the rise of Islam in the 7th century, the Red Sea gained even greater significance in global trade. Islamic merchants, known as the "Mariners of Islam," utilized the Red Sea and its connecting routes to establish commercial networks extending from East Africa to the Indian subcontinent. Muslim traders from Arabia, Persia, and the Indian Ocean region flocked to cities like Mecca and Medina, which became vibrant trade hubs. From there, goods were transported across the Red Sea to reach markets in the Mediterranean, connecting the Muslim world with distant economies.

During the Islamic Golden Age, these trade links expanded further, with the Abbasid Caliphate promoting and protecting maritime commerce in the Red Sea. The ports of Aden and Jeddah flourished as commercial centers, attracting merchants from across the Islamic world. The Red Sea became a melting pot of different cultures, languages, and religions, contributing to the vibrant cosmopolitanism of the region.

European powers also recognized the importance of the Red Sea as a gateway to the lucrative markets of the East. During the Age of Exploration, the Portuguese sought control over key strategic ports along the Red Sea, such as Hormuz and Aden. These ports allowed them to secure their dominance in the spice trade, enabling them to bypass the Ottoman-controlled routes through the Mediterranean. Later, European colonial powers like the British and French also sought to control access to the Red Sea as part of their imperial ambitions, leading to the establishment of colonies and naval bases along its coast.

In modern times, the Red Sea continues to play a vital role in global trade. It remains an essential route for maritime transportation, particularly for the shipping of oil, gas, and other resources from the Gulf countries and Africa to consumers around the world. The Suez Canal, a marvel of engineering completed in 1869, further enhances the Red Sea's importance by providing a direct link for vessels to bypass the longer journey around the Cape of Good Hope. The canal revolutionized global trade, reducing travel time and costs, and greatly facilitating commerce between the East and the West.

The economic significance of the Red Sea is not limited to its role as a transportation route. The sea's rich marine resources have supported local communities for centuries, with fishing being a crucial activity. The Red Sea boasts diverse coral reefs, mangrove forests, and seagrass beds that provide habitats for numerous marine species. However, overfishing, destructive fishing practices, and pollution have threatened the delicate ecological balance of the Red Sea. Efforts are being made to promote sustainable fishing and protect these valuable marine resources, ensuring their preservation for future generations.

Furthermore, the seabed of the Red Sea holds the potential for mineral resources, fueling interest in mining activities. Potassium, phosphates, and manganese nodules are among the valuable resources found in the Red Sea. However, the extraction of these minerals must be approached with caution, utilizing responsible and sustainable practices to minimize environmental impacts and preserve the delicate ecosystem of the region.

The security and stability of the Red Sea region are crucial for uninterrupted trade. Geopolitical dynamics in the area have become increasingly complex in recent years, with conflicts such as the ongoing war in Yemen and political instability in Sudan posing challenges to regional security. Piracy, terrorism, and arms smuggling have emerged as serious threats, necessitating international cooperation to ensure the safety of maritime trade routes and the stability of the region.

In conclusion, the Red Sea's historical and contemporary significance in global trade is profound. As a vital maritime route connecting different continents and cultures, it has been instrumental in the exchange of goods, ideas, and people throughout history. From ancient civilizations to the modern global economy, the

Red Sea's impact on trade and cultural exchange cannot be overstated. By understanding the complexities of this strategic waterway, we gain a deeper appreciation for the interconnectedness of our world and the importance of preserving the Red Sea for future generations.

B. RECENT INCREASE IN ATTACKS - GEO-POLITICAL TENSIONS, PIRACY, AND RE-GIONAL CONFLICTS

The Red Sea region has experienced a concerning surge in attacks on commercial ships, which has raised alarm bells among global stakeholders. These attacks can be attributed to several factors, including geopolitical tensions, piracy, and regional conflicts that have plagued the area.

Geopolitical tensions play a significant role in the recent increase in attacks in the Red Sea. The region is a convergence point for various rivalries and conflicts involving states and non-state actors. Countries such as Iran, Saudi Arabia, Egypt, and Israel have long-standing regional power struggles and ideological differences.

These tensions have intensified over the years, leading to increased hostility and proxy wars.

One of the primary geopolitical tensions in the Red Sea region stems from the rivalry between Saudi Arabia and Iran. Both countries compete for influence and seek to maintain dominance in the Persian Gulf and the wider Middle East. This power struggle has escalated to a point where the Red Sea has become a battleground for these regional powerhouses, with each side supporting proxy groups in Yemen, Somalia, and other nearby countries. This volatile environment has provided an opportunity for attacks on commercial ships, as these actors aim to assert their control and exert pressure on their adversaries.

Furthermore, Egypt's relation with Ethiopia adds to the complexity of the geopolitical landscape in the Red Sea. Ethiopia's construction of the Grand Ethiopian Renaissance Dam on the Blue Nile, a key tributary of the Nile River, has sparked tensions with downstream countries like Egypt and Sudan. Egypt, heavily dependent on the Nile's water resources, views the dam as a threat to its national security and has expressed its concerns on multiple occasions. The potential for an escalation of tensions between Egypt and Ethiopia could further exacerbate the security risks in the Red Sea region.

Piracy is another major contributor to the rise in attacks. The Red Sea has a long history of piracy dating back centuries, and despite efforts to combat it, piracy remains a persistent problem. Somalian pirates, in particular, have been known to target commercial ships passing through the Red Sea, seizing vessels and holding crews hostage for ransom. These attacks not only pose a significant threat to the safety of maritime trade but also have broader implications for regional stability.

The roots of piracy in the Red Sea can be traced to Somalia's state collapse in the early 1990s. With no functioning government or law enforcement, pirate groups emerged and took advantage of the vast Somali coastline to launch attacks on passing ships. These pirates, equipped with high-speed vessels and sophisticated weapons, have posed a grave menace to maritime security. Over the years, international efforts, such as naval patrols and collaborations with regional governments, have been implemented to combat piracy in the region. However, these efforts have faced challenges due to a lack of effective governance and economic opportunities in Somalia.

Regional conflicts in the Red Sea area have also played a role in the recent increase in attacks. Ongoing civil wars in Yemen, Libya, and Syria, combined with territorial disputes between neighboring countries, have created a volatile environment conducive to maritime insecurity. In these conflict zones, different factions, militias, and terrorist groups often resort to acts of piracy and attacks on commercial ships to fund their activities or disrupt their adversaries.

The civil war in Yemen, in particular, has escalated tensions in the Red Sea. The conflict between the Houthi rebels and the internationally recognized government, backed by a Saudi-led coalition, has resulted in a dire humanitarian crisis. The Houthis have targeted maritime traffic passing through the Bab el Mandeb strait, a vital shipping route connecting the Red Sea to the Gulf of Aden, triggering concerns about the safety of commercial vessels and international trade.

The strategic importance of the Red Sea's major maritime chokepoints, such as the Bab el Mandeb strait and the Suez Canal, adds another layer of vulnerability. The narrow and easily navigable shipping routes make them attractive targets for those seeking to disrupt global trade or exert control over key transit points. The location of the Red Sea, linking the Mediterranean Sea to the Indian Ocean, further enhances its geopolitical significance, as any disturbance here can have cascading effects on global economic activities.

The recent increase in attacks in the Red Sea poses significant challenges beyond the immediate safety of maritime vessels. It has the potential to disrupt global oil supplies, increase transportation costs, and slow down international trade. These consequences can have ripple effects on various industries and economies worldwide, considering the Red Sea's vital role as a key trade route for an array of commodities.

Efforts to address this crisis require a comprehensive approach that encompasses diplomatic negotiations, international collaboration, and enhanced security measures. To effectively tackle the problem, it is crucial for regional and global powers to address the under-lying geopolitical tensions, counter piracy activities, and contribute to resolving regional conflicts. A holistic and coordinated response is necessary to ensure the safety of the Red Sea and maintain stability in global maritime trade.

Additionally, the environmental factors in the Red Sea region have also contributed to the rise in attacks. The Red Sea is known for its rich biodiversity and coral reef ecosystems, which attract divers, researchers, and tourists from around the world. However, climate change, pollution, and overfishing have put enormous pressure on these fragile ecosystems. The degradation of marine resources has resulted in the loss of livelihoods for coastal communities, fuelling economic desperation and reinforcing the cycle of piracy.

Furthermore, the abundance of international ship-ping traffic passing through the Red Sea makes it an attractive target for criminal activities. Cargo ships carrying valuable goods, including oil, gas, and other commodities, present lucrative opportunities for illicit actors. The prospect of seizing these vessels, hijacking their cargo, or demanding hefty ransoms has incentiv-ized pirates and other criminals to operate in the region.

In response to the growing security challenges, var-ious international naval forces have conducted patrols and provided escorts for commercial ships in the Red Sea. The Combined Maritime Forces (CMF), a multi-national coalition comprising naval assets from multiple countries, has been committed to combating piracy and ensuring the safety of maritime trade. Similarly, the European Union Naval Force's Operation Atalanta has conducted counter-piracy operations in the region since 2008. These efforts have significantly reduced the number of successful piracy attacks, demonstrating the effectiveness of coordinated multinational operations.

However, piracy and attacks on commercial ships continue to persist due to the complex and multifaceted nature of the problem. Addressing these challenges requires a comprehensive approach that goes beyond military responses. Strengthening governance, promoting economic development, and cultivating stable political systems in countries such as Somalia and Yemen are essential for long-term solutions.

Additionally, regional cooperation and dialogue among Red Sea countries are crucial for enhancing maritime security. Sharing intelligence, coordinating patrols, and establishing joint mechanisms for responding to threats can considerably contribute to a safer Red Sea. Encouraging investment in coastal communities and providing alternative livelihoods for potential pirates can help break the cycle of violence and create a more secure environment.

Moreover, international organizations, such as the United Nations, have a vital role to play in supporting regional efforts to address security challenges in the Red Sea. By facilitating diplomatic dialogue, providing resources, and coordinating multilateral initiatives, the international community can contribute to finding sustainable solutions to the root causes of piracy and attacks.

In conclusion, the recent surge in attacks on commercial ships in the Red Sea region is a complex issue influenced by geopolitical tensions, piracy, regional conflicts, and environmental factors. Efforts to address these challenges must encompass diplomatic negotiations, international collaboration, enhanced security measures, and long-term solutions to the underlying causes. ByBy implementing a comprehensive approach, it is possible to ensure the safety of the Red Sea and maintain stability in global maritime trade. Diplomatic negotiations play a crucial role in resolving the geopolitical tensions that contribute to the insecurities in the region. Engaging in dialogue and seeking diplomatic resolutions can help ease tensions and reduce the incentive for attacks on commercial ships.

International collaboration is also essential in addressing the security challenges in the Red Sea. Cooperation between regional and global powers can enhance intelligence sharing, coordinate patrols, and develop joint response mechanisms to threats. Multinational naval operations, such as the Combined Maritime Forces, have proven effective in combating piracy and ensuring the safety of maritime trade. Increasing collaboration and support for such initiatives can contribute to a safer Red Sea.

In addition to addressing the immediate security

concerns, it is crucial to focus on the underlying causes of piracy and attacks on commercial ships. Strengthening governance and creating stable political systems in countries like Somalia and Yemen can help reduce the prevalence of violent activities. Providing economic development opportunities and alternative livelihoods for coastal communities can break the cycle of piracy and reduce the incentive for criminal activities.

Furthermore, protecting and preserving the Red Sea's fragile ecosystems is crucial for long-term sustainability. Efforts to combat climate change, reduce pollution, and promote sustainable fishing practices can help restore the marine resources and livelihoods of coastal communities. Supporting initiatives for marine conservation and raising awareness about the importance of preserving biodiversity can contribute to a more secure and resilient Red Sea.

International organizations, such as the United Nations and regional bodies like the Arab League and the African Union, should play an active role in supporting the efforts of Red Sea countries. These organizations can facilitate diplomatic dialogue, provide resources, and coordinate multilateral initiatives to address the security challenges in the region. By working together, the international community can contribute to finding sustainable solutions and ensuring the long-term stability of the Red Sea.

In conclusion, the surge in attacks on commercial ships in the Red Sea region is a multifaceted issue influenced by geopolitics, piracy, regional conflicts, and environmental factors. Efforts to address this crisis require a comprehensive approach that encompasses diplomatic negotiations, international collaboration, enhanced security measures, and long-term solutions to the underlying causes. By working together, regional and global stakeholders can ensure the safety of the Red Sea and maintain stability in global maritime trade.

C. STRATEGIC IMPORTANCE OF THE BAB EL MANDEB STRAIT

The Bab el Mandeb strait, known in Arabic as "The Gate of Tears," has long been a focal point of global attention due to its strategic importance. Nestled between the Arabian Peninsula and the Horn of Africa, this narrow passageway serves as a vital link between the Red Sea and the Gulf of Aden. Spanning only 18 miles at its narrowest point, the Bab el Mandeb strait holds immense economic, geopolitical, and security significance, attracting the interest of major powers throughout history.

From an economic perspective, the Bab el Mandeb strait plays a crucial role in facilitating international trade. It serves as a key transit route for maritime commerce, connecting Europe, Asia, and the Middle East. The sheer volume of goods transported through this waterway is staggering. Each day, more than 10% of the world's seaborne oil trade passes through its narrow confines. This equates to approximately 4.8 million barrels of oil, originating from resource-rich nations such as Saudi Arabia, Iran, Iraq, and other Gulf countries, and destined for various regions across the globe. The strait also enables the transportation of natural gas, military equipment, and consumer goods, serving as a vital conduit for global supply chains. Any disruption to the smooth flow of trade through the Bab el Mandeb strait would have far-reaching consequences, leading to increased shipping costs, volatility in energy prices, and potential disruptions to global markets.

Beyond its economic significance, this narrow waterway has significant geopolitical implications. The Bab el Mandeb strait is strategically positioned, linking vital international waterways such as the Suez Canal and the Strait of Hormuz. Given its role in the global trade network, controlling or influencing the strait has been a longstanding endeavor for various powers. Throughout history, empires and nations have recognized the advantages of holding sway over this critical passage. The Ottoman Empire, for example, sought control over the Bab el Mandeb strait as it expanded its influence in the Red Sea region. Similarly, during the era of British colonial rule, the British Empire recognized the importance of this maritime route and established naval bases to maintain control.

In recent times, the United States has displayed significant interest in the Bab el Mandeb strait. Acting as a global superpower, the U.S. aims to ensure freedom of navigation and protect vital shipping routes in the region. Recognizing its strategic value, the U.S. maintains a military presence in the area, including naval support and intelligence operations, to safeguard its interests and regional stability. With the rise of global powers and shifting geopolitical dynamics, the Bab el Mandeb strait has become an arena of competition, both overt and subtle, reflecting the broader struggles for influence that shape global affairs.

Moreover, the Bab el Mandeb strait's geographic location makes it susceptible to regional conflicts and security threats. Recent unrest in Yemen, situated near the strait, has amplified concerns regarding the security of this vital waterway. The Houthi rebels, who control parts of Yemen where the strait is located, have periodically posed threats to disrupt or even block the passage through their control of coastal areas. Such actions not only have direct repercussions on regional stability but also carry broader implications for global trade and security.

International efforts have been made to safeguard the security and stability of the Bab el Mandeb strait. Collaborative endeavors between navies, seafaring nations, and regional organizations aim to combat piracy, smuggling, and other transnational crimes that pose threats to maritime security. By improving surveillance capabilities, conducting joint patrols, and facilitating information sharing, these initiatives seek to maintain the free and safe navigation of this critical waterway. Furthermore, the Bab el Mandeb strait's security is closely intertwined with broader regional concerns, such as the ongoing conflicts in Yemen and the Horn of Africa. Addressing the underlying roots of instability in these areas is essential to secure the stability and economic prosperity that rely on the unimpeded flow of trade through the strait.

In conclusion, the Bab el Mandeb strait stands as a testament to the interconnectedness of the global community. Its economic significance, serving as a conduit for the transportation of oil, natural gas, and other goods, highlights its essential role in the modern world economy. Simultaneously, the strategic location of the strait attracts the attention of major powers, who vie for influence and control over this critical passageway. Ensuring the security and stability of the Bab el Mandeb strait is not only crucial for the nations in the region but also for the global community. Collaborative efforts to combat security threats and address underlying conflicts are necessary to maintain open, safe, and efficient trade routes, fostering peace and prosperity for all those who depend on this vital gateway.

D. VULNERABILITY OF GLOBAL ENERGY SUPPLY CHAINS TO DISTURBANCES IN THE RED SEA REGION

The Red Sea region serves as a critical hub for global energy supply chains, particularly for oil and natural gas. Its strategic position, connecting key energy-producing nations in the Middle East with major consumption centers across the globe, makes it a focal point for ensuring the stability and security of the world's energy supply. However, this region is characterized by unique geographic, political, and socio-economic factors that introduce significant challenges and potential vulnerabilities.

One of the primary concerns revolves around the vulnerability of oil tankers and cargo ships navigating the Red Sea. In recent years, incidents of piracy and attacks on commercial vessels have escalated, causing alarm among energy exporters and importers alike. These acts of piracy, combined with armed conflicts and geopolitical tensions in the area, pose a direct threat to the safety of ships and the uninterrupted transportation of oil and other energy resources.

The Bab el Mandeb strait, located at the southern

entrance of the Red Sea, plays a crucial role. Serving as a vital transit point for ships traveling to and from the Suez Canal, it connects Asia, Europe, and the Americas. Any disruption in the flow of oil through this narrow strait would force ships to seek alternative routes, resulting in longer and costlier journeys. These alterations could potentially lead to increased transportation costs, negatively impacting both producers and consumers and contributing to potential price hikes. Thus, any disturbances in the Bab el Mandeb strait can have far-reaching ramifications for global energy markets.

Furthermore, the Red Sea region is home to several critical oil-producing nations such as Saudi Arabia, Yemen, and Sudan. The presence of armed conflicts, political instability, and other potential disturbances in these countries create vulnerabilities in oil production levels. Any disruption in oil production from these nations could result in supply shortages and further price volatility in the global market.

In addition to these immediate risks, the vulnerability of the Red Sea region extends beyond local impacts. Various countries heavily rely on oil and natural gas reserves in this area, incorporating it into their energy diversification strategies. Consequently, disturbances or disruptions in the Red Sea region could impede these diversification efforts, leaving countries vulnerable to energy shortages and price shocks. The reliance on a single region for energy resources underscores the need for diversification and resilience in global energy supply chains.

Moreover, the interconnected nature of global energy supply chains means that disturbances in the Red Sea region can have cascading effects worldwide. Significant disruptions in the flow of oil or natural gas through the Red Sea could trigger increased competition for resources in other regions, intensifying strain on existing supply chains. Moreover, this competition could potentially drive up prices further, impacting global energy consumers across multiple sectors. The ripple effect highlights the complex and interdependent nature of the global energy market, necessitating a comprehensive approach to address vulnerabilities in the Red Sea region.

Ensuring the stability and security of energy supply chains in the Red Sea region requires a collaborative effort involving nations and international organizations. Strengthening maritime security mechanisms, such as naval patrols, surveillance systems, and international collaboration against piracy, can help deter potential threats and safeguard commercial vessels. Additionally, promoting diplomatic initiatives to resolve regional conflicts, address political instability, and foster cooperation between nations is crucial for minimizing potential disruptions.

Investing in alternative energy transportation routes can also play a significant role in mitigating vulnerabilities. Developing pipelines, expanding liquefied natural gas (LNG) infrastructure, and diversifying transportation options can reduce dependence on the Red Sea region and enhance the resilience of global energy supply chains. Exploring alternative energy sources, such as renewables, and promoting energy efficiency measures can further decrease dependence on fossil fuels, offering greater energy security and sustainability.

In conclusion, the vulnerability of global energy supply chains to disturbances in the Red Sea region is a complex and multifaceted challenge. Addressing the risks posed by piracy, armed conflicts, and geopolitical tensions requires a comprehensive approach involving maritime security measures, diplomatic initiatives, and investments in alternative energy transportation routes. Strengthening the resilience and security of energy supply chains in the Red Sea region will not only ensure the stability of the global energy system but also contribute to global energy security and sustainable development.

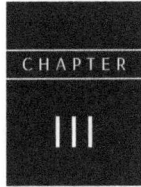

EFFECTS ON THE COST OF OIL

Geopolitical Implications

The Red Sea crisis has significant geopolitical implications, as it involves multiple regional and global players with varying interests. The competition for influence and control in the region adds another layer of complexity to the already volatile situation. Understanding the geopolitical dynamics at play is crucial to comprehending the broader ramifications of the crisis.

1. **Regional Power Struggles:**

- Saudi-Iran Rivalry: The ongoing rivalry between Saudi Arabia and Iran, the two major regional powers, plays a central role in shaping the dynamics of the Red Sea crisis. Both countries vie for influence over Yemen, and their support for opposing factions exacerbates the conflict's intensity. A sectarian dimension also underlies this rivalry, as Saudi Arabia is predominantly Sunni Muslim, while Iran is predominantly Shia Muslim.
- Saudi Arabia and Egypt Partnership: Saudi Arabia's close relationship with Egypt further complicates the situation in the Red Sea region. Egypt's control over the Suez Canal, which connects the Red Sea to the Mediterranean Sea, is strategically important for both trade and military purposes. Consequently, Saudi Arabia seeks to strengthen its ties with Egypt to secure its own interests and maintain influence in the region.
- Gulf Cooperation Council (GCC): The Red Sea crisis has implications not only for Saudi Arabia but also for other members of the GCC, such as the United Arab Emirates, Kuwait, Bahrain, Oman, and Qatar. These countries share concerns about the stability and security of the Red Sea region, especially considering their reliance on oil exports and the importance of secure maritime trade routes for their economies.

1. **International Actors:**

- United States: The involvement of international actors, particularly the United States, adds another dimension to the geopolitical landscape of the Red Sea crisis. The U.S. considers the region strategically important due to its economic and security interests. The U.S. maintains a military presence in the area, primarily to combat terrorism and protect its allies, including Saudi Arabia and Israel.
- China: China's growing influence in the Red Sea region is of significant geopolitical importance. As the world's largest crude oil importer, China heavily relies on stable oil supplies from the Middle East. Ensuring the safety of maritime routes is crucial for China's energy security and economic development, prompting the country to take a keen interest in the stability of the Red Sea region.
- European Union (EU): The EU, primarily as a consumer of Middle Eastern oil, also has economic and energy security interests in the region. The Red Sea crisis increases the EU's concerns about access to oil and its impact on energy prices. The EU may seek to support diplomatic efforts and contribute to stability in the region to safeguard its interests.

1. **Proxy Conflicts and External Influences:**

- Proxy Conflicts: The Red Sea crisis serves as a battleground for proxy conflicts between various regional and global powers. Yemen is a prime example, with regional actors providing support to warring factions. This exacerbates the conflict and prolongs the instability, as these external powers fuel the internal divisions and prevent a resolution.

- Militant Groups and Terrorism: The crisis in the Red Sea region creates a fertile ground for militant groups, such as Al-Qaeda and the Islamic State (ISIS), to exploit the chaos and expand their operations. These groups take advantage of ungoverned spaces and weak state institutions to pursue their ideological goals, posing a direct threat to regional stability and global security.

- Maritime Security: The Red Sea crisis raises concerns about the security of maritime trade routes that are vital for global trade and energy transportation. Piracy, smuggling, and illegal activities flourish in areas of instability, jeopardizing international commerce and the safety of seafarers. Stakeholders must collaborate to enhance maritime security frameworks to address these challenges effectively.

1. **Humanitarian and Human Rights Concerns:**

- Humanitarian Crisis in Yemen: The crisis in the Red Sea region has contributed to a severe humanitarian crisis in Yemen. The conflict has resulted in widespread displacement, loss of life, and the collapse of basic services. Humanitarian organizations face significant challenges in providing aid due to the ongoing violence and limited access to affected areas.
- Human Rights Violations: The Red Sea crisis also highlights human rights violations committed by warring parties. Civilians in Yemen suffer from indiscriminate bombings, blockades, and grave human rights abuses. The international community and human rights organizations must address these violations and hold the responsible actors accountable.

In conclusion, the Red Sea crisis carries profound geopolitical implications due to regional power struggles, the involvement of international actors, proxy conflicts, and human rights concerns. Understanding the complex dynamics at play is crucial in addressing the crisis effectively and finding long-term solutions. Collaboration and diplomacy among all stakeholders are essential to stabilize the region, ensure the security of maritime trade routes, alleviate the humanitarian crisis, and promote peace and stability in the Red Sea and its surrounding areas.

A. IMPACT OF THE RED SEA ISSUE ON THE GLOBAL OIL MARKET

The impact of the Red Sea issue on the global oil market has engendered a deep sense of concern and apprehension within the international community. Historically, the Red Sea region has served as a pivotal hub for the transportation of oil, underscoring its strategic significance. This essential maritime route facilitates the movement of millions of barrels of oil each day from major oil producers in the Middle East to global markets, particularly Europe and Asia. The intricate network of vessels plying these waters ensures the uninterrupted flow of oil, sustaining economies worldwide.

Central to the concerns surrounding the Red Sea issue is the iconic Bab el Mandeb strait, which stands as a testament to both the opportunities and vulnerabilities within the global oil trade. This narrow passage marks the southern entrance to the Red Sea, nestled between the Arabian Peninsula and the Horn of Africa.

Its location is of immense importance, as it offers oil tankers the expeditious route to the Suez Canal and the Mediterranean Sea, thereby securing access to European markets. Alternatively, ships can navigate towards the Indian Ocean and Asian markets. The sheer magnitude of oil volumes transported through this critical conduit illustrates its irreplaceable role in the global energy landscape.

Regrettably, recent years have witnessed a series of developments that have set alarm bells ringing regarding the stability and security of the Red Sea region. The emergence of increasing geopolitical tensions, a persistent piracy threat, and acts of terrorism have conspired to exacerbate concerns surrounding the vulnerability of this vital maritime corridor. The possibility of disruptions in the transportation of oil through the region poses a significant risk to global energy security. Any severe interruption could consequently trigger a domino effect on the availability and cost of oil in international markets. In turn, this would lead to a surge in oil prices, reverberating across various industries and causing widespread impact on consumers worldwide.

Furthermore, it is crucial to acknowledge the interdependencies that link the Red Sea issue with the nearby Strait of Hormuz, an additional critical chokepoint for global oil transportation. Located at the entrance to the Persian Gulf, the Strait of Hormuz is a nerve center that commands crucial strategic importance in the global oil trade. As such, any disturbances or conflicts in either the Red Sea region or the Strait of Hormuz could un-leash a chain reaction, amplifying supply disruptions and exacerbating the consequences for global oil sup-plies. Given the already precarious nature of the Strait of Hormuz, such an eventuality would have dire and far-reaching consequences for the stability of global energy resources.

The reverberations of the Red Sea issue extend beyond the realm of oil, encompassing other vital commodities essential for global trade. Natural gas, minerals, and agricultural products are also transported through the Red Sea region, lending it a multifaceted and pivotal role in the global supply chain. When disruptions occur in this maritime conduit, delays in the delivery of these in-dispensable commodities are inevitable. The ensuing lo-gistical challenges significantly increase transportation costs and further disrupt global supply chains, creat-ing adverse effects on various industries and ultimately impacting the global economy.

Nevertheless, stakeholders in the maritime industry recognize the urgency of mitigating risks associated with the Red Sea issue and are taking proactive measures in response. Maritime companies are diligently reviewing their shipping routes and augmenting security protocols to minimize vulnerabilities. These measures include increased surveillance, enhanced deterrence measures, and close collaboration with naval forces deployed in the region. While such proactive approaches are commend-able, they come at a cost. Longer alternative routes or the necessity for additional security personnel and equipment raise operational expenses for maritime companies. Consequently, these increased costs may be passed on to consumers, amplifying the economic impacts of the Red Sea issue.

In conclusion, the Red Sea issue looms large as a formidable threat to the global oil market and beyond. Any interruption in this crucial maritime route poses severe consequences for global oil supplies, potentially leading to price hikes and disruptions across various industries. The interconnected nature of the Red Sea region with other critical energy routes underscores the pressing need for immediate attention and concerted efforts by the international community to ensure stability in this vital area. Failure to address this issue promptly could have far-reaching consequences on global energy security and economic stability.

B. CONCERNS ABOUT POSSIBLE INTER- RUPTIONS TO OIL EXPORTS

The recent uptick in attacks on commercial ships in the Red Sea has raised significant concerns about potential interruptions to oil exports. The Red Sea region, bordered by countries such as Saudi Arabia, Egypt, Sudan, and Yemen, serves as a vital maritime route for transporting oil from the Middle East to Europe and Asia. These concerns arise from the vulnerability of oil tankers navigating through the Red Sea and the Bab el Mandeb strait, a narrow passage connecting the Red Sea to the Gulf of Aden and the Arabian Sea. The strategic importance of this route cannot be overstated, as a substantial portion of the world's oil supplies pass through these waters.

The attacks on commercial ships in the Red Sea represent diverse threats, ranging from piracy to sabotage. Maritime piracy has long been a concern in this region, with criminal elements taking advantage of the geopolitical instability, weak governance, and lawlessness in countries along the coast. Pirates often target ships, including oil tankers, to hijack or loot valuable cargo or to demand hefty ransom payments. These acts of piracy not only endanger the lives of crew members but also disrupt international trade and inflict financial losses on shipping companies.

Moreover, sabotage constitutes another grave concern in the Red Sea. Acts of sabotage can involve covert operations, such as the placement of mines or explosive devices on commercial ships or infrastructure, with the aim to disrupt or damage vessels and their cargo. These intentional acts of sabotage have the potential to cause significant harm to the affected ships and pose a threat to the overall security and stability of oil transportation in the region.

The potential for interruptions to oil exports from the Red Sea has raised concerns among both producing and consuming nations. Oil-producing countries, such as Saudi Arabia and Egypt, heavily rely on stable and secure shipping routes to maintain their economies and fulfill their contractual obligations to global oil markets. Disruptions in these routes could result in a significant reduction in revenue and economic stability for these nations. For instance, in 2018, an attack on two Saudi oil tankers near the Bab el Mandeb strait temporarily disrupted oil shipments, leading to a brief surge in oil prices.

On the other hand, oil-consuming countries world-wide have significant stakes in the smooth flow of oil exports from the Red Sea. Any disruption in oil supplies from this region has the potential to cause price shocks that can reverberate through various sectors of their economies. Higher oil prices can lead to increased production costs, transportation expenses, and energy bills, affecting businesses and households alike. Moreover, elevated oil prices can also contribute to inflationary pressures and impact the affordability of essential goods and services.

Furthermore, the Red Sea crisis amplifies existing concerns about the security of other critical maritime routes, notably the nearby Strait of Hormuz. This narrow channel, located between Iran and Oman, is the most important global chokepoint for oil transportation, through which one-third of global oil supplies pass. Given the proximity of the Red Sea and the Strait of Hormuz, disturbances in one area can quickly have ripple effects on the other. The interconnectedness of these strategic routes poses significant risks to global energy security and intensifies concerns about potential disruptions in oil exports.

To mitigate these concerns, international efforts are underway to enhance security measures in the Red Sea region. The United Nations, the international naval coalition Combined Maritime Forces, and regional organizations, such as the Red Sea and Gulf of Aden Commission (RSGA), are working to improve maritime security through increased patrols, intelligence sharing, and capacity building efforts. Additionally, coastal states in the area have been urged to strengthen their naval capabilities and enhance their cooperation to combat piracy and safeguard oil transportation.

However, finding a long-term solution to ensure the safety of oil transportation remains a complex challenge amid ongoing geopolitical tensions and conflicts. The Red Sea region, like many other maritime hotspots, is afflicted by various armed conflicts and political instability, making it vulnerable to criminal activities and acts of sabotage. Addressing the root causes of these conflicts and establishing sustainable peace and stability are crucial steps towards securing the Red Sea and safeguarding global energy supply chains.

In recent years, several factors have contributed to the increase in attacks on commercial ships in the Red Sea. The ongoing conflict in Yemen, with Houthi rebels launching missile attacks at Saudi Arabia and targeting commercial vessels, has significantly raised the level of risk in the region. The Houthis have access to surface-to-sea missiles, posing a direct threat to oil tankers passing through these waters. Additionally, the presence of other armed groups, such as Somali pirates and terrorist organizations like Al-Qaeda and ISIS, adds further complexity to the security situation.

Another factor exacerbating the concerns about oil exports in the Red Sea is the growing influence of non-state actors in the region. Yemen's coast, for example, has become a hotspot for illegal arms trafficking, as various armed rebel groups seek to fund their activities through illicit means. The availability of advanced weapons in the hands of these non-state actors increases the potential for attacks on commercial ships and oil infrastructure. These groups often exploit the porous borders and weak enforcement capabilities of coastal states, making it challenging to curb these illicit activities.

Moreover, the Red Sea region's vulnerability to environmental disasters also poses a threat to oil exports. Oil spills, whether accidental or deliberate, can have devastating consequences on the marine ecosystem and shipping operations. For instance, the spillage of oil from grounded or sabotaged vessels can affect the surrounding sea lanes, hindering navigation and negatively impacting marine life. The proximity of coral reefs and ecologically sensitive areas in the Red Sea further emphasizes the need for stringent regulations and preventive measures to minimize the environmental impact of potential oil-related incidents.

Efforts to address the security risks and potential interruptions to oil exports in the Red Sea must go beyond solely enhancing naval patrols and fortifying defenses. It is crucial to establish comprehensive maritime governance frameworks that promote regional cooperation, information sharing, and intelligence coordination. This includes fostering agreements among coastal states to combat piracy, enhance maritime law enforcement capabilities, and enact robust legal frameworks to prosecute those engaged in criminal activities.

Furthermore, addressing the underlying conflicts and political instability in the region is essential for long-term security. Diplomatic efforts should be intensified to find peaceful resolutions and encourage dialogue among warring factions. Regional powers and the international community need to collaborate to support conflict resolution initiatives, offer humanitarian aid, and provide assistance for post-conflict reconstruction. Strengthening governance institutions and promoting economic development can contribute to greater stability in the Red Sea region and reduce the incentives for criminal activities such as piracy and sabotage.

In conclusion, concerns about possible interruptions to oil exports due to the crisis in the Red Sea region are substantial, necessitating comprehensive strategies to secure shipping routes and safeguard global energy supply chains. The vulnerability of these vital maritime routes to piracy, sabotage, armed conflicts, and non-state actors underscores the need for immediate and sustained international cooperation. Strengthening maritime security capabilities, addressing root causes of conflicts, and fostering regional cooperation are essential components of a multifaceted approach to ensure the uninterrupted flow of oil exports from the Red Sea.

C. POTENTIAL SHARP RISE IN OIL PRICES DUE TO DISRUPTIONS IN MAJOR SHIPPING ROUTES

The recent increase in attacks on commercial ships in the Red Sea raises grave concerns about potential disruptions in major shipping routes, particularly those crucial for oil transportation. The interconnected nature of global trade means that any disruption in these routes could have significant consequences for global oil prices, resulting in widespread economic implications. In order to understand the potential ramifications of such disruptions, it is important to delve deeper into the factors at play.

1. Dependency on maritime transportation: Most of the world's oil is transported via maritime routes, highlighting the critical role that shipping plays in the global energy trade. The Red Sea, with its strategic location connecting major oil-producing countries in the Middle East to global markets, has become a vital passage for oil shipments. Approximately 10% of global seaborne crude oil and refined product exports pass through this region, making it a vital lifeline for the energy needs of nations worldwide.

   · The reliance on maritime transportation for oil is not solely due to the efficiency and cost-effectiveness of shipping, but also the lack of alternative infrastructure in certain regions. Landlocked countries or those lacking pipeline connections heavily rely on seaborne trade to fulfill their energy demands. Additionally, the flexibility of shipping allows for oil to be transported to diverse destinations based on market demand, adding another layer of complexity to the global energy trade.

1. Vulnerability of critical shipping routes: The Bab el Mandeb strait, situated at the southern entrance of the Red Sea, is a vulnerable chokepoint

due to its narrow width of just 29 kilometers. This narrow waterway is a crucial transit route for vessels carrying oil from the Persian Gulf to the Suez Canal, hence making it a prime target for potential disruptions.

· The recent increase in attacks by Houthi rebels on commercial ships and oil infrastructure in the Red Sea has revealed the susceptibility of shipping routes to such threats. These attacks, which include missile strikes, naval mines, and maritime ambushes, pose a significant risk to the safe and efficient passage of oil tankers through these waters. The Houthis' ability to deploy advanced weaponry, often acquired from external sources, further amplifies concerns regarding the security of these critical shipping routes.

· Moreover, the geographical proximity of the Red Sea to other turbulent regions, such as the Gulf of Aden and the Strait of Hormuz, introduces further vulnerabilities. Any escalation of conflict or disruptions in one of these regions can easily spill over into others, compounding the risks associated with global oil transportation.

1. Impact on oil prices: Disruptions in major shipping routes can have a profound impact on oil prices due to the sheer magnitude of crude oil shipments passing through these areas. Any significant

disruption that hampers the flow of oil from the Middle East to global markets would inevitably result in reduced supply. This imbalance between supply and demand would likely lead to a sharp increase in oil prices.

· Furthermore, the interconnectedness of global energy markets means that a disruption in one region could have a cascade effect on other parts of the world. For instance, the closure of the Bab el Mandeb strait would force the redirection of oil shipments towards alternative routes, potentially congesting other chokepoints such as the Strait of Hormuz or the Cape of Good Hope. These congestion points can further exacerbate supply constraints and elevate oil prices worldwide.

· The impact on oil prices would not only affect end consumers but also have significant repercussions for oil-exporting nations. Countries heavily reliant on oil revenues can experience fluctuations in their fiscal budgets, affecting government expenditure and economic stability. Thus, disruptions in major shipping routes can trigger a ripple effect throughout the global economy.

1. Economic implications: Higher oil prices due to disruptions in major shipping routes have far-reaching economic implications, impacting various sectors and nations.

- Industries heavily reliant on oil, such as transportation, manufacturing, and agriculture, may face increased production costs. These increased costs can have a direct impact on consumer prices, potentially leading to higher inflation rates. As a result, consumer spending power can diminish, affecting individual households and overall economic growth.

- Moreover, countries heavily dependent on oil imports may face significant challenges due to rising energy costs. Governments often subsidize oil prices for their citizens, and if these subsidies become unsustainable, it can strain fiscal budgets and pose a threat to economic stability. Countries with limited alternative energy sources may be particularly vulnerable in such scenarios.

- In addition to the direct economic consequences, disruptions in major shipping routes can also lead to heightened market uncertainty. The oil market is heavily influenced by speculation and investor sentiment, which can exacerbate price volatility. Increased uncertainty can impact financial markets, investment decisions, and global trade flows, compounding the economic implications of disruptions in major shipping routes.

1. Interconnected risks: The interconnected nature of global shipping routes means that disruptions in one region can have a cascading effect on

others. The Red Sea region is not an isolated entity, and any escalation of conflicts or disruptions in its waters can have implications for neighboring waterways.

- For example, the Strait of Hormuz, located at the entrance of the Persian Gulf, is another critical bottleneck for oil transportation. Approximately 20% of the world's oil supply passes through this narrow strait, making it as vital as the Bab el Mandeb for global energy security. If disruptions occur simultaneously in both the Red Sea and the Persian Gulf, it can severely constrain global oil supplies and send shockwaves throughout the energy markets, leading to even higher oil prices and heightened market volatility.

- The interconnected risks extend beyond the immediate economic sphere and into the realm of geopolitics. Major powers, including the United States, China, and Russia, show significant interest in ensuring access to vital shipping routes for their economic and strategic interests. Disruptions in major shipping routes can heighten tensions and trigger geopolitical rivalries, potentially exacerbating conflicts and affecting regional security dynamics. The consequences of these interconnected risks have the potential to reverberate globally, impacting international relations and diplomatic alliances.

Efficiently addressing the potential sharp rise in oil prices due to disruptions in major shipping routes requires a multifaceted approach, involving the collaboration of regional and global actors. International cooperation in deploying security measures, such as enhanced surveillance, intelligence sharing, and maritime patrols, becomes imperative to ensure the safety and security of vital trade routes.

Furthermore, diversification of energy sources and transportation routes can help reduce dependencies on vulnerable regions. The development of alternative energy sources, such as renewable energy, and investment in other transportation modes, such as pipelines and rail networks, can provide greater resilience and minimize the potential impact of disruptions in major shipping routes.

Efforts towards efficient diplomacy and conflict resolution mechanisms are key to addressing the underlying geopolitical tensions in the Red Sea region. Engaging in dialogue, promoting peaceful resolutions, and fostering regional cooperation can contribute to the stability of the region, ensuring uninterrupted global energy supply chains and averting further economic upheaval.

By focusing on a multi-faceted approach encompassing security, diversification, and diplomacy, the global community can work towards mitigating the potential risks posed by disruptions in major shipping routes. This will not only help maintain stability in global oil markets but also preserve the overall health of the world economy.

D. INTERCONNECTED RISKS WITH THE NEARBY STRAIT OF HORMUZ AND THEIR IMPACT ON GLOBAL OIL SUPPLY

The Red Sea crisis has significant interconnected risks with the nearby Strait of Hormuz, which can have a tremendous impact on global oil supply. Located between the Persian Gulf and the Gulf of Oman, the Strait of Hormuz is a critical shipping route through which a substantial portion of the world's oil passes.

As tensions rise in the Red Sea region, it raises concerns about the potential for disruptions in the Strait of Hormuz. Any instability or conflict that affects the Red Sea can have a ripple effect on the global oil market through its impact on this crucial chokepoint.

The Strait of Hormuz is responsible for the transportation of around 21 million barrels of oil per day, accounting for approximately 21% of global oil consumption. This vital waterway is strategically located, connecting the energy-rich Persian Gulf—home to major oil-producing countries such as Saudi Arabia, Iraq, Iran,

Kuwait, and the United Arab Emirates—to key global markets.

Situated at the entrance of the Arabian Gulf, the Strait of Hormuz is a narrow passage, with a width of only about 21 miles at its narrowest point. This geographical constraint makes it vulnerable to disruption, whether due to conflicts, acts of sabotage, or blockades.

In recent years, the Strait of Hormuz has become a hotspot for tensions among regional powers. Iran, in particular, has threatened to close the Strait if its interests are compromised. In 2019, Iran seized several oil tankers passing through the Strait, escalating tensions with the United States and other Western powers. The incident highlighted the unpredictable nature of the situation and the potential for further disruption.

The global significance of the Strait of Hormuz is undeniable. Its closure, even if temporary, would have immediate and far-reaching consequences. Oil prices would skyrocket, potentially quadrupling or more within days. The knock-on effects on the global economy would be severe, leading to higher transportation costs, inflation, and reduced consumer spending.

The strait's strategic importance extends beyond its role as an oil passageway. It is also crucial for the transportation of liquefied natural gas (LNG) and other key commodities, serving as a vital artery for international trade. Approximately one-fifth of the world's LNG passes through this narrow channel, connecting the energy-rich countries of Qatar and Iran with major consumers in Asia and Europe. Therefore, any disruptions in the Strait of Hormuz would not only impact energy markets but also have wider implications for global supply chains and trade flows.

While efforts have been made to reduce dependence on the Strait of Hormuz, diversifying transportation routes and energy sources on a global scale is challenging. Alternative pipelines, such as the East-West pipeline in Saudi Arabia or the proposed Trans-Arabian Pipeline, offer potential routes bypassing the Strait. However, political and logistical obstacles have hindered progress in these endeavors. Additionally, regional conflicts and rivalries have made it difficult to establish alternative transportation corridors that ensure a reliable and secure flow of energy.

The intensified conflicts and risks in the Red Sea and the Strait of Hormuz underscore the need for international cooperation and multilateral approaches to ensure stability and secure global oil supply. Bilateral and multilateral dialogues should focus on easing tensions, resolving disputes, and preventing further escalation. Building trust and establishing diplomatic channels can play a vital role in reducing the likelihood of accidents or miscalculations that could trigger a full-blown crisis.

International organizations such as the United Nations and regional bodies like the Gulf Cooperation Council (GCC) should facilitate dialogue and mediate conflicts to prevent further destabilization and ensure freedom of navigation. Moreover, naval patrols from multinational forces can help deter hostile actions and ensure the safe passage of vessels through sensitive waterways like the Strait of Hormuz.

The global energy market must also continue to invest in technological advancements, such as increased use of renewables and energy efficiency measures, to reduce the reliance on oil and enhance energy security. By diversifying sources of energy and reducing the demand for oil, countries can mitigate the risks associated with disruptions in the Strait of Hormuz and the Red Sea region. This includes supporting research and development efforts in alternative energy technologies, incentivizing clean energy transitions, and promoting energy conservation practices.

In conclusion, the interconnected risks between the Red Sea and the nearby Strait of Hormuz pose significant challenges to global oil supply and the stability of the global economy. The potential for disruptions in the Strait, whether due to conflicts, acts of sabotage, or blockades, necessitates a comprehensive approach to safeguarding vital shipping routes and maintaining stability. Regional and international cooperation, diplomatic efforts, and investments in alternative energy sources are crucial to prevent the escalation of tensions and ensure the uninterrupted flow of global oil supply. Emphasizing renewable energy solutions and energy conservation will further enhance energy security and provide a pathway towards a more sustainable and resilient future.

MORE GENERAL
CONSEQUENCES FOR
INTERNATIONAL TRADE

———————————

Further Impacts on International Trade

The Red Sea crisis has unleashed a cascade of multi-faceted factors that continue to reverberate throughout the realm of international trade. While much attention has been focused on the implications for oil prices, it is imperative to delve even deeper into the wider conse-quences that extend beyond the energy sector. Serving as a vital trade route for an array of commodities, in-cluding minerals, manufactured goods, and agricultural products, any disruptions in the Red Sea region bear significant weight on global trade dynamics and necessitate a comprehensive analysis of their far-reaching impacts.

One of the immediate consequences brought about by the Red Sea crisis is the onset of shipping delays, which ripple through the entire supply chain. Heightened security measures, the rerouting of vessels, and the unsettling occurrence of attacks on commercial ships all contribute to the prolonged transit times of goods passing through the region. To navigate the challenges posed by the crisis, companies are compelled to allocate substantial additional resources, leading to increased shipping costs. For businesses operating on tight margins, these heightened expenses can be burdensome, potentially leading to price hikes for consumers.

Furthermore, piracy remains a persistent issue in the Red Sea region, threatening not only lives but also international trade. Acts of piracy not only cause physical harm to seafarers but also pose a significant threat to global economic stability. Shipowners and operators are compelled to resort to costly security measures such as the hire of armed guards or investments in cutting-edge technologies to deter pirates. These additional expenses can be detrimental to the financial viability of shipping companies, subsequently impeding their competitiveness in the global market.

The unpredictable nature of the Red Sea crisis also engenders uncertainty surrounding the safety of vessels, cargo, and crew. Shipping companies and insurers meticulously consider these risks when determining freight rates, resulting in increased maritime insurance costs. Ultimately, these expenses are often passed on to consumers, leading to higher prices for imported goods and potentially dampening demand.

The instability in the Red Sea region not only affects shipping and logistics but also disrupts global supply chains, which in turn impacts numerous industries worldwide. Companies that rely heavily on resources or goods from countries situated in the Red Sea region face difficulties in obtaining necessary inputs, leading to production delays or cost overruns. This disruption can have far-reaching consequences, resulting in reduced production output, job losses, and potential recessions in some cases.

Furthermore, The Red Sea crisis underscores the urgent need for companies to reassess their operational strategies, including the possibility of diversifying their supply chains. In seeking alternative routes altogether, businesses explore options such as the Cape of Good Hope or the Panama Canal to mitigate risks related to the Red Sea region. However, these alternative routes often entail extended transit times, increased fuel consumption, and elevated transportation costs. Consequently, consumers may experience delayed deliveries and higher prices for imported goods.

From a geopolitical standpoint, the Red Sea crisis possesses ramifications that surpass immediate trade disruptions. The involvement of major global powers such as the United States, Russia, Iran, and Saudi Arabia further complicates the situation as their interests converge or diverge in relation to the region. The complex web of rivalries and conflicts within the Red Sea region necessitates nuanced diplomacy and comprehensive international cooperation to foster stability, as any escalation in tensions could further amplify the risks to global trade and regional security.

It is crucial for the international community to acknowledge the intrinsic interconnectivity of global trade and the underlying risks associated with disruptions in vital maritime routes. A timely and effective resolution of the Red Sea crisis is imperative to safeguard the stability of international trade and safeguard geopolitical alliances. Failure to address the root causes and develop sustainable long-term solutions could have far-reaching consequences, not only for international trade but also for the political stability and security of the Red Sea region and beyond.

A. BEYOND OIL: IMPORTANCE OF THE RED SEA FOR VARIOUS COMMODITIES

The Red Sea holds a diverse and complex role in the global trade landscape, serving as a critical conduit for a wide range of commodities. Its strategic location connects the Mediterranean Sea to the Indian Ocean, creating a vital maritime route that facilitates the exchange of goods between East and West. The Red Sea region boasts major ports and trading hubs, making it an indispensable link in the global supply chain.

While oil is undoubtedly a significant commodity transported through the Red Sea, numerous other resources hold immense value and reliance on this crucial waterway. Let us delve deeper into these commodities and their importance:

Natural gas, being cleaner and more environmentally friendly than other fossil fuels, has gained increasing importance in the global energy market. The Red Sea region plays a pivotal role in the trade of natural gas. Egypt, with its vast offshore reserves, has become a major producer and exporter. It operates liquefied natural gas (LNG) terminals and receives shipments from neighboring countries such as Equatorial Guinea and Nigeria, which are then re-exported through the Red Sea. The Red Sea's stable route ensures the secure transportation of natural gas to meet global energy demands.

Similarly, Israel has discovered significant offshore natural gas reserves in the Mediterranean, and the Red Sea provides a crucial link for its exports. The Leviathan field, one of the world's largest natural gas finds in recent years, relies on the Red Sea as a transportation route to reach international markets, contributing to Israel's energy independence and regional stability.

Saudi Arabia, as the largest producer of oil in the world, also relies on the Red Sea for the export of natural gas. With ambitious plans to diversify its energy mix, the kingdom has been investing heavily in the production of natural gas. The Red Sea provides a convenient and cost-effective passage for Saudi Arabia's natural gas exports, strengthening its position as a global energy player.

Beyond natural gas, the Red Sea region plays a pivotal role in the transportation of various minerals and metals. High-quality iron ore, an essential component in the steel industry, is produced in countries like Sudan and Ethiopia. These landlocked nations heavily depend on the Red Sea as it provides a crucial link to export their iron ore to global markets. The Red Sea's extensive coastal infrastructure and efficient shipping routes facilitate the transportation of iron ore, enabling these countries to connect with global markets and contribute to the global steel industry.

Furthermore, the Red Sea's significance extends to precious minerals like gold and copper. Sudan, in particular, boasts rich gold deposits and is one of the world's largest exporters of the precious metal. The Red Sea provides a crucial gateway for Sudan's gold exports, connecting them to lucrative markets worldwide. The region's stability and secure trade routes are vital for ensuring the continuous flow of gold and other precious minerals, supporting international trade and fostering economic growth.

Copper, a vital resource for industries ranging from electronics to construction, is also exported through the Red Sea. Eritrea and Yemen, amongst others, are significant copper-producing countries in the region. The Red Sea's accessibility ensures the efficient transportation of copper, contributing to international trade and fostering economic opportunities for these nations.

In addition to natural resources, the Red Sea is a critical trade route for agricultural commodities. Countries like Egypt, Saudi Arabia, and Sudan rely on the Red Sea for the export of their agricultural produce. Egypt's fertile lands along the Nile River and Sudan's irrigated agricultural schemes provide a diverse array of fruits, vegetables, and staple crops such as wheat and rice. The Red Sea ports serve as gateways for the transportation of these agricultural commodities, ensuring reliable food supplies globally and supporting local economies.

Moreover, the Red Sea region's abundant marine resources support a thriving fishing industry. Sudan, Yemen, and Djibouti have well-established fishing sectors, heavily reliant on the Red Sea's waters. The sea's ports provide access to wider market opportunities for fresh fish and seafood, meeting global demand and supporting the livelihoods of local communities.

It is also important to highlight that the Red Sea serves as a crucial trade route for manufactured goods. The region's connectivity and accessibility make it a vital connecting point for goods produced in Asia, Europe, and Africa. Goods ranging from electronics, textiles, and automotive components to machinery and chemicals pass through the Red Sea ports, facilitating global trade and contributing to economic growth worldwide.

Understanding the depth and importance of the Red Sea in facilitating the trade of various commodities is crucial for the international community. The stability and security of this maritime route are of utmost importance to ensure the continuous flow of goods and support global economies. Collaborative efforts among nations, enhanced security measures, and diplomatic engagement are necessary to safeguard the Red Sea network, ensuring its stability and preserving its vital role in facilitating international trade.

B. POTENTIAL CONSEQUENCES OF SHIPPING DELAYS, HIGHER TRANSPORTATION COSTS, AND A SLOWDOWN IN INTERNATIONAL TRADE

Shipping delays, higher transportation costs, and a slowdown in international trade have the potential to trigger a series of profound consequences that go far beyond immediate economic impacts. The Red Sea region, situated strategically as a major trade route and a connector between key economic centers, is particularly significant in these occurrences, necessitating a thorough examination of the deeper implications that can arise as a result.

One of the critical consequences of shipping delays is the disruption of global supply chains. In today's highly interconnected world, numerous industries rely on just-in-time delivery systems, where the efficient flow of materials and goods is essential for seamless production processes. Any delays in shipping through the Red Sea can lead to shortages of key components, undermining productivity and causing bottlenecks in manufacturing operations. This disruptive domino effect permeates the entire supply chain, resulting in reduced economic output and growth, with increased risks of inflation and decreased business confidence affecting markets around the globe.

Higher transportation costs emerge as another significant consequence of disturbances in the Red Sea region. When faced with risks or conflicts, shipping companies may be compelled to reroute vessels or resort to longer alternative routes, which consequently incur additional expenses such as increased fuel consumption and prolonged journey times. Furthermore, heightened security measures implemented in response to piracy threats or regional conflicts contribute to higher insurance premiums and security charges. These amplified costs are often transferred to consumers, leading to rising prices for goods and services, which, in turn, can dampen consumer spending and constrain economic growth both domestically and internationally.

The repercussions extend beyond economic factors, encompassing social and political consequences as well. A slowdown in international trade, facilitated by the Red Sea, triggers a ripple effect on economies dependent on global trade for sustained growth and development. Reduced trading activities result in diminished exports and imports, negatively affecting revenue streams and employment opportunities. This economic downturn can erode social stability, leading to increased unemployment rates, which, in turn, breed social unrest and political instability. Governments, grappling with reduced tax revenues, may be limited in their ability to fund social programs or infrastructure projects, hindering progress and exacerbating social and economic inequality.

Moreover, disturbances in the Red Sea region can contribute to regional tensions and entrench existing conflicts, with potential spill-over effects across neighboring zones. The interplay of economic adversity, political instability, and limited resources may intensify social grievances and heighten the risks of violence and extremism. This volatility jeopardizes the safety and well-being of local populations, while simultaneously impeding regional integration and cooperation, hindering efforts to foster peace and mutual understanding.

Addressing the potential consequences of disruptions

in the Red Sea necessitates a comprehensive and coordinated approach involving governments, international organizations, and maritime stakeholders. Collaboration is vital for developing robust security measures that ensure the safety of vessels and the swift flow of goods. Implementing cutting-edge technologies such as vessel tracking and communication systems, along with shared intelligence and resources, can significantly combat piracy and other criminal activities, securing global trade routes.

Furthermore, it is essential to diversify trade routes and promote the development of alternative transportation networks to mitigate risks associated with a single vulnerable chokepoint. By unlocking the full potential of existing alternative routes, such as the Suez Canal or the Cape of Good Hope, reliance on the Red Sea can be decreased, creating a more resilient global trade network.

In the long term, efforts must be focused on addressing the underlying causes of instability in the Red Sea region. Promoting peace and stability through diplomatic initiatives, investing in economic development programs, and supporting local initiatives that address the root causes of conflicts can pave the way for sustainable growth and prosperity. By engaging with local communities, fostering education and access to employment opportunities, and ensuring equitable resource distribution, the region can build a foundation for stability and mutual cooperation.

In conclusion, the potential consequences of disruptions in the Red Sea, such as shipping delays, higher transportation costs, and a slowdown in international trade, have far-reaching implications that extend beyond the surface-level economic impacts. The interconnectedness of global economies exacerbates the effects of such disruptions, affecting industries, economies, and societies worldwide. Recognizing the urgency of the situation, collaborative efforts are necessary to ensure the uninterrupted flow of goods and safeguard the stability of the Red Sea region. By addressing both immediate challenges and underlying issues, we can strive to preserve the integrity of international trade and promote sustainable economic prosperity for all.

C. MARITIME COMPANIES REEVALUATING ROUTES AND SECURITY PROTOCOLS, LEADING TO INCREASED OPERATIONAL COSTS

Maritime companies around the world have been forced to extensively reevaluate their shipping routes and security protocols in light of the escalating crisis in the Red Sea region. The increasing frequency and audacity of attacks on commercial vessels have sparked significant concern within the industry, prompting companies to acknowledge the heightened risks and costs associated with operating in these troubled waters.

One of the immediate consequences for maritime companies is the need to find alternative shipping routes that either bypass the Red Sea altogether or minimize their exposure to potential threats. Companies have been compelled to thoroughly analyze the geopolitical dynamics, threat assessments, and patterns of piracy in the region to make informed decisions about their shipping routes. This analysis includes tracking the activities of organized pirate groups, understanding their modus operandi, and identifying the hotspots most prone to attacks. By gaining a deeper understanding of the challenges, companies can strategically plan their routes and defenses.

This reevaluation process involves consultations with international organizations, governmental bodies, and maritime industry stakeholders. Collaborative efforts allow for the sharing of intelligence, accurate risk assessments, and the development of comprehensive strategies to counter piracy and maritime terrorism. The exchange of information supports a coordinated response, ensuring that companies receive the most up-to-date guidance on best practices and security measures.

The decision to alter shipping routes also requires a careful assessment of the economic and environmental implications. Companies must weigh the potential risks of operating in the Red Sea against the financial costs and environmental impacts of longer, alternative routes. These longer voyages often mean increased fuel consumption, additional transportation costs, and extended transit times. Such disruptions can result in delays in the delivery of goods, affecting the stability of supply chains and straining relationships between shipping companies and their clients. The economic ramifications extend beyond the shipping industry, with potential cascading effects on various sectors reliant on timely and efficient maritime transportation.

To mitigate the risks associated with operating in the Red Sea region, maritime companies have been compelled to enhance their security protocols. This includes investing in advanced technologies that facilitate real-time monitoring and early detection of potential threats. Thermal imaging cameras, drones, and satellite surveillance systems enable companies to gain a comprehensive understanding of their surroundings, helping them detect suspicious activities and respond swiftly to any potential security breaches.

Vessel hardening measures play a crucial role in safeguarding vessels and their crew. Installation of physical barriers such as razor wire and electrified fences impede unauthorized access, while water cannons can ward off would-be attackers. Additionally, companies are implementing security drills and training programs for their crews, enabling them to respond effectively and decisively in the event of an attack. Through these measures, maritime companies are actively deterring pirate attacks and safeguarding the lives of their crew members.

The deployment of well-trained armed guards has become a widely adopted practice among maritime companies operating in high-risk areas. The presence of armed guards on board not only serves as a visible deterrent but also acts as a crucial last line of defense in the event of an attack. However, the use of armed guards is a contentious issue, as various legal complexities and jurisdictional differences surround these practices. Companies must navigate these legal intricacies and ensure that their security measures comply with international laws and sanctions.

The reevaluation of routes and security protocols has substantial financial implications for maritime companies. In addition to increased fuel costs and transportation expenses associated with longer routes, higher insurance premiums are often required to cover the escalated risks. Companies must allocate budgets for the procurement of advanced security technologies and equipment, as well as ongoing training and maintenance. For smaller shipping companies with limited resources, these additional costs can be particularly burdensome and potentially impact their competitiveness in the market.

Furthermore, the redirection of vessels and the subsequent congestion in alternative shipping routes can have far-reaching consequences for global trade. Delays in maritime transportation not only disrupt supply chains and increase logistics costs but can also have a ripple effect on various industries reliant on timely and reliable deliveries. Manufacturing operations may be hindered due to a lack of essential components, retailers may face shortages of goods, and consumers may experience price fluctuations and limited availability of certain products.

The reevaluation of routes and security protocols is an ongoing challenge for maritime companies operating in the Red Sea region. With the crisis showing no signs of abating, companies must continually assess the risks and threats in close collaboration with international organizations, governments, and maritime stakeholders. Sharing intelligence, coordinating naval patrols, and developing comprehensive strategies to counter piracy and maritime terrorism are crucial for ensuring the safety of vessels and the stability of global trade.

In conclusion, the escalating crisis in the Red Sea region has forced maritime companies to extensively reevaluate their shipping routes and security protocols. This decision comes with numerous complexities, including the need to find alternative, longer routes that bypass the troubled area and the associated challenges of increased fuel consumption and transportation costs. The deployment of enhanced security measures such as vessel hardening, advanced surveillance technologies, and armed guards further adds to operational expenses. These financial burdens have an industry-wide impact, with smaller companies struggling to absorb the additional costs. Moreover, the congestion in alternative shipping routes and delays in maritime transportation pose wider consequences for global trade, affecting supply chains, manufacturing, retail, and consumers alike. As the crisis unfolds, it is imperative for maritime companies to remain vigilant, adapt their strategies, and strengthen international cooperation efforts to secure the safety of their vessels and the stability of global commerce.

GLOBAL POWER
STRUCTURES

The Red Sea region is a highly volatile geopolitical landscape characterized by a multitude of factors that contribute to the current crisis and shape the power dynamics in the area. At the heart of these dynamics lies the complex and deep-rooted rivalry between Iran and Saudi Arabia, driven by religious, political, and economic ideologies.

The Iranian-Saudi rivalry dates back to the Islamic Revolution in 1979, which resulted in Iran's transformation into an Islamic republic and ignited a sense of revolutionary zeal that posed a challenge to the conservative Sunni monarchies in the region, particularly

Saudi Arabia. The ideological divide between the Shia-dominated Iran and the predominantly Sunni Arab countries reinforced existing sectarian tensions and exacerbated divisions within the Muslim world.

The sectarian dimension of the rivalry between Iran and Saudi Arabia has further fueled the conflicts and tensions in the Red Sea region. Iran, a predominantly Shia nation, has sought to expand its influence by supporting Shia communities in neighboring countries, such as Lebanon, Iraq, Bahrain, and Yemen. This has been perceived as a direct threat by Saudi Arabia, which views itself as the leader of the Sunni Muslim world and has historically sought to counter Iran's influence.

Yemen has emerged as the battleground for the Iranian-Saudi rivalry. The conflict in Yemen first erupted in 2014 when Houthi rebels, who are aligned with Iran, seized control of the capital, Sana'a, and ousted the internationally recognized Yemeni government. Saudi Arabia, fearing Iran's growing influence on its southern border, spearheaded a military coalition with regional allies to support the Yemeni government and counter the Houthi rebels. This intervention has further escalated and prolonged the conflict, turning Yemen into a humanitarian catastrophe and amplifying regional tensions.

Beyond the Iranian-Saudi rivalry, territorial disputes and power vacuums continue to shape the power structures in the Red Sea region. Somalia, an unstable state plagued by internal conflicts and a lack of centralized authority, remains a hotspot for regional and international power struggles. Factors such as piracy, terrorism, illegal fishing, and smuggling have flourished in Somalia, attracting various non-state actors and further destabilizing the region. These dynamics have drawn in external players vying for control of Somalia's natural resources and influence over its government.

Proxy wars and foreign interventions are also prominent features of the Red Sea region's power dynamics. The involvement of major global players, including the United States, Russia, Iran, and Saudi Arabia, has further complicated the situation. The United States maintains a significant military presence in the region, primarily to safeguard the security of global trade routes and counter terrorism. Russia, on the other hand, has capitalized on opportunities presented by the ongoing conflicts in Syria and Yemen and has expanded its presence in the Red Sea region to challenge American dominance and project its own geopolitical interests.

Moreover, control over strategic chokepoints has become paramount for power projection and economic dominance in the Red Sea region. The Suez Canal, a vital international waterway connecting the Mediterranean Sea to the Red Sea, enables ships to bypass the treacherous Cape of Good Hope, providing faster access between Europe and Asia. Around 10% of global trade passes through this route, making it a strategic asset for states and non-state actors alike. Similarly, the Bab el Mandeb strait, located at the southern entrance to the Red Sea, serves as a critical gateway for maritime trade between the Middle East, Africa, and Europe, particularly for oil shipments. The control of these chokepoints allows states and non-state actors to manipulate global trade, project military power, and secure their economic interests in the region.

In summary, the power structures in the Red Sea region revolve around historical rivalries, long-standing tensions, proxy wars, and foreign interventions. The competition for regional dominance between Iran and Saudi Arabia, conflicts like the civil war in Yemen, and territorial disputes shape the current crisis. Additionally, the control over strategic chokepoints, such as the Suez Canal and the Bab el Mandeb strait, becomes instrumental in projecting power and ensuring economic advantages. Resolving the crisis and establishing stability in the Red Sea region necessitates a comprehensive understanding of these complex power dynamics, accompanied by a commitment from global powers to prioritize cooperation, diplomacy, and the long-term security of the region.

A. OVERVIEW OF REGIONAL ANIMOSITIES, LONG-STANDING TENSIONS, AND INTERNATIONAL POWER STRUGGLES

The Red Sea region has long been a theater of regional animosities, deep-rooted tensions, and international power struggles. These complex dynamics have had far-reaching consequences on the stability of the region, exacerbating the crisis in the Red Sea and impeding efforts to achieve lasting peace.

Historical Animosities in the Red Sea Region:

The origins of the animosities in the Red Sea region can be traced back centuries, with various historical factors fueling the tensions that persist today. One of the most prominent historical dividing lines in the region is the Sunni-Shia divide. This deep-seated religious divide between Saudi Arabia, as the leader of Sunni Islam, and Iran, as the leading Shia power, has served as a catalyst for conflict and regional power struggles.

The rivalry between Saudi Arabia and Iran dates back to the 16th century and has been characterized by competition over religious authority, political influence, and control over strategic resources. This rivalry has historical roots in the different interpretations of Islam and the contest between the Sunni Ottoman Empire and the Shia Safavid Empire. Over time, this deep-rooted rivalry has evolved into a broader competition for regional hegemony, with both countries seeking to secure allies, expand influence, and weaken each other's positions.

The sectarian nature of this rivalry has been

exacerbated by geopolitical factors. The overthrow of the Shah of Iran in 1979 and the rise of the Islamic Republic under Ayatollah Khomeini marked a turning point in Shia ascendancy. The Iranian revolution and its anti-Western stance threatened the political and economic interests of Sunni states, particularly Saudi Arabia. This intensification of ideological and geopolitical competition has had a destabilizing effect on the region, with proxy conflicts and support for opposing factions fueling tensions in countries like Iraq, Syria, Yemen, Lebanon, and Bahrain.

Other historical tensions within the Red Sea region stem from contests over territory and resources. Egypt and Sudan, for example, have historically disputed the ownership of the Hala'ib Triangle, a territory located in a border area between the two countries. Proximity to the Red Sea, its maritime resources, and its importance as a trading hub have made the region a focal point for territorial disputes. Such disputes not only strain bilateral relations but also have wider implications for regional stability.

Power Struggles and Proxy Wars in the Red Sea:

In addition to historical animosities, the Red Sea region has become the stage for various power struggles between global and regional actors, further complicating its stability. The United States, as a major global power, has long been involved in the region primarily due to its interests in countering terrorism and ensuring the free flow of commerce. Its military presence in Djibouti, the only permanent U.S. military base in Africa, underscores its commitment to projecting power in the Red Sea region.

Similarly, Russia has increasingly engaged with the Red Sea region due to both economic and geopolitical interests. The Russian intervention in the Syrian conflict, characterized by its support for the government of President Bashar al-Assad, has significantly impacted the balance of power in the region. Russia's naval base in Tartus, Syria, enables it to project power in the Eastern Mediterranean and impact the dynamics of the Red Sea.

China's interest in the Red Sea is primarily driven by its ambitious Belt and Road Initiative (BRI), which envisions enhanced connectivity and trade between China and the rest of the world. The Red Sea's strategic location and its proximity to Africa's emerging markets make it a significant area of interest for China. As part of the BRI, China has invested in infrastructure projects, such as ports and transportation networks, to strengthen its economic ties with countries in the region. Its naval presence in the Red Sea and its establishment of a military base in Djibouti further illustrate its strategic objectives.

The impact of these power struggles and foreign interventions is profound. They have exacerbated existing regional conflicts and complicated efforts to achieve peace. Countries like Yemen, Libya, and Sudan have emerged as battlegrounds for proxy wars, with different regional and international powers supporting opposing factions. The influx of weapons and foreign fighters prolongs these conflicts, undermines regional stability, and creates breeding grounds for extremist groups such as Al-Qaeda and ISIS.

Consequences of the Regional Instability:

The regional animosities and power struggles have had severe consequences for the stability and security of the Red Sea region. Commercial ships passing through the Red Sea face various risks, including attacks from armed groups, piracy, and disruptions due to ongoing clashes between rival forces. These risks not only threaten the safety of maritime trade but also drive up transportation costs, impacting global economic activities due to increased insurance premiums and delays.

Furthermore, the protracted conflicts and power struggles have disrupted social cohesion, exacerbating human suffering and leading to large-scale refugee and humanitarian crises. Countries like Yemen and Sudan are grappling with severe humanitarian emergencies, with millions of people displaced and in need of urgent assistance.

Finding a Path Towards Stability:

Resolving the complex challenges of the Red Sea region requires concerted efforts at multiple levels. It demands a comprehensive understanding of the historical, political, and religious dynamics at play. Regional actors must acknowledge and address the underlying issues driving animosities to create an atmosphere conducive to dialogue and reconciliation. International actors should commit to supporting diplomatic efforts and fostering cooperation rather than exacerbating divisions for their own strategic gains.

Inclusive and mediated negotiations must be pursued to resolve ongoing conflicts and address underlying grievances. Regional organizations such as the Gulf Cooperation Council (GCC), the Arab League, and the African Union (AU) can play pivotal roles in facilitating dialogue and finding diplomatic solutions. Multilateral initiatives, like the United Nations-led peace processes, can help coordinate international efforts and provide a platform for all parties involved to address grievances, find compromises, and work towards sustainable peace.

In conclusion, the Red Sea region finds itself entangled in a web of historical animosities, power struggles, and proxy wars. The complex dynamics driven by regional rivalries, international interventions, and historical disputes continue to exacerbate the crisis in the Red Sea. Achieving lasting peace and stability necessitates a multilateral approach, where stakeholders acknowledge and address the root causes of conflicts, foster co-operation, and prioritize the well-being of the region's people.

B. INFLUENCE OF CIVIL WARS, TERRI-TORIAL DISPUTES, AND POWER VACUUMS ON THE RED SEA REGION

The Red Sea region has long been plagued by a multitude of civil wars, territorial disputes, and power vacuums, all of which have had far-reaching consequences for its stability and security. These conflicts have aggravated the already precarious situation, transforming the region into a hotspot of tension and aggression, with ripple effects felt beyond its borders.

Civil wars in countries such as Yemen, Sudan, and Somalia have had a profound impact on the Red Sea region. In Yemen, the ongoing conflict between Houthi rebels and the Yemeni government, supported by a Saudi-led coalition, has resulted in a catastrophic humanitarian crisis. The displacement of millions of people not only disrupts their lives but also places a strain on neighboring countries that are hosting refugees, such as Djibouti and Saudi Arabia. The limited resources available in these countries are stretched thin, exacerbating the precarious living conditions of both refugees and host communities. Additionally, the civil war has created a power vacuum that terrorist groups like Al-Qaeda in the Arabian Peninsula (AQAP) and the Islamic State (IS) have exploited, allowing them to expand their presence and carry out attacks, further destabilizing the region and threatening international security.

In Sudan, the protracted civil war in the Darfur region has caused immense suffering and displacement. The conflict, triggered by long-standing grievances and re-source-based tensions, has led to hundreds of thousands of deaths and the uprooting of millions of people from their homes. This humanitarian catastrophe destabi-lizes not only Sudan but also neighboring countries like South Sudan, which experienced its own civil war after gaining independence in 2011. The interplay between these conflicts exacerbates regional security concerns, as the movement of armed groups, flow of weapons, and refugee flows are difficult to contain, continuing to fuel instability.

Somalia has been grappling with prolonged civil war and a chronic absence of effective central governance. The power vacuum resulting from the collapse of the central government in 1991 allowed various armed fac-tions, warlords, and extremist groups like Al-Shabaab to gain control over territories and expand their influence. These groups have exploited the weakened state struc-tures to engage in acts of piracy, terrorism, and other criminal activities. The instability in Somalia directly affects its neighboring countries, particularly Kenya, which has suffered numerous attacks by Al-Shabaab militants, leading to loss of life, displacement, and economic setbacks.

Territorial disputes in the Red Sea region have also contributed to its instability. The Hanish Islands, located in the southern Red Sea, have been a subject of contention between Yemen and Eritrea for decades. Conflicting claims over the islands' sovereignty, which are believed to have rich fishing and potential hydrocarbon resources, have periodically led to naval clashes and intermittent armed confrontations. These incidents have escalated tensions between the two countries, further straining diplomatic relations. Another area of contention is the Red Sea Triangle, a region claimed by Egypt, Sudan, and Saudi Arabia. The overlapping territorial claims and ongoing disputes over maritime boundaries have heightened the risk of armed conflict and strained regional relationships. Resolving these disputes through peaceful means is crucial to reducing tensions and fostering stability in the Red Sea region.

Maritime border disputes have also accentuated regional tensions and hindered cooperation in the Red Sea. Eritrea and Djibouti have been embroiled in military confrontations over their shared maritime boundaries, resulting in casualties and strained diplomatic relations. Control over these waters has significant economic implications, as they facilitate trade, fishing activities, and potential exploration of offshore resources. Ongoing disputes hamper efforts to maintain the security and stability of Red Sea shipping lanes, which are vital for global trade. The heightened risks associated with maritime border tensions have increased insurance costs, disrupted supply chains, and discouraged foreign investments, weakening the region's economic prospects.

Power vacuums resulting from regime changes have also left a void in leadership and governance, creating fertile ground for conflict and exploitation. In Yemen, the power vacuum that emerged when the Houthi rebels seized control of the capital, Sana'a, allowed outside powers to intervene in the conflict. Iran's support for the Houthis and Saudi Arabia's intervention on behalf of the Yemeni government turned the civil war into a proxy battle, further escalating tensions in the Red Sea. The involvement of external actors only perpetuates and prolongs the conflict, with devastating consequences for the civilian population and regional stability.

The influence of civil wars, territorial disputes, and power vacuums on the Red Sea region cannot be underestimated. The resulting instability and insecurity have affected not only the countries directly involved but also neighboring nations and international actors with interests in the region. They disrupt trade routes, hinder economic development, and perpetuate cycles of poverty and underdevelopment. Furthermore, these conflicts have created an environment conducive to the spread of radical ideologies, terrorism, and transnational criminal activities. The Red Sea's proximity to the European continent and its strategic position linking the Middle East, Africa, and Asia make it vulnerable to the spill-over of extremism, as well as the smuggling of weapons, drugs, and humans across its shores.

Addressing these complex issues and finding peace-ful resolutions is crucial to restoring stability, safeguard-ing vital trade routes, and promoting economic growth in the Red Sea region. Regional and international actors must come together to support sustainable peace initi-atives, strengthen governance structures, and promote socio-economic development. These efforts should also prioritize addressing the root causes of conflicts, such as grievances over political representation, access to resources, and ethnic tensions. Only through compre-hensive and inclusive strategies can the Red Sea region recover from its current state of instability and build a more secure and prosperous future.

C. PROXY WARS AND FOREIGN INTER-VENTIONS EXACERBATING THE CRISIS

Proxy wars and foreign interventions continue to wreak havoc in the Red Sea region, deepening the crisis and further destabilizing the already fragile balance of power. The conflicts in Yemen, Syria, and the broader Middle East have contributed significantly to the region's turmoil, but it is crucial to analyze the role of external actors and examine their motivations and strategies.

Saudi Arabia's motivations for intervening in Yemen go beyond merely countering Iranian influence. The Kingdom seeks to protect its southern border and maintain its regional dominance. Yemen's strategic location, bordering the Red Sea and the Arabian Sea, gives it access to crucial international shipping routes, making it a significant maritime chokepoint. Saudi Arabia, dependent on oil exports, is keen on ensuring the security of these vital sea lanes and preventing any threat to its economic interests.

Moreover, Yemen's proximity to Saudi Arabia's southern border poses a direct security threat. The Houthi rebels, who control substantial portions of Yemen, have repeatedly targeted Saudi cities and infrastructure with ballistic missiles and drones. These attacks not only cause significant damage but also highlight the vulnerability of Saudi Arabia and its strategic assets. Saudi Arabia's intervention in Yemen is, therefore, driven by national security concerns and the need to maintain stability in its immediate neighborhood.

Iran, on the other hand, views the conflict in Yemen as an opportunity to expand its regional influence and challenge Saudi Arabia's dominance. The widened sectarian divide between Sunni-majority Saudi Arabia and Shia-majority Iran compounds the geopolitical rivalry between the two powers. By supporting the Houthi rebels, Iran aims to achieve several objectives: undermine Saudi Arabia's position as the guardian of Sunni interests, establish a foothold in the Arabian Peninsula, and exert pressure on its regional rival.

The United States has its own complex motivations for involvement in the Red Sea region. Historically, American security interests in the region have revolved around the protection of its allies, ensuring the freedom of navigation, and countering terrorism. Yemen's instability and the rise of militant groups like Al-Qaeda in the Arabian Peninsula (AQAP) pose direct threats to American national security. Failing states and ungoverned spaces provide fertile grounds for extremist groups to flourish, making it imperative for the U.S. to engage in counterterrorism efforts and prevent these groups from expanding their reach.

Furthermore, the United States is concerned about the flow of weapons into the region, particularly those supplied to the Houthi rebels by Iran. Arms proliferation exacerbates conflicts and poses long-term risks to regional stability. Hence, the U.S. has implemented arms embargoes to curtail these illicit transfers, in an attempt to prevent further escalation of violence.

Russia's increased presence in the region, particularly through its involvement in Syria, has added another layer of complexity to the Red Sea crisis. Russia's strategic objectives in Syria revolve around the protection of its longstanding ally, the Assad regime, and the preservation of its military bases and naval access. Syria's Mediterranean coastline provides Russia with a vital warm-water port, ensuring its continued projection of power in the region.

Furthermore, Russia's intervention in Syria presents an opportunity for the Kremlin to showcase its military capabilities and expand its arms export market. Successful combat operations involving sophisticated weaponry demonstrate Russia's capabilities to potential buyers, reinforcing its position as a global arms exporter. By establishing a military presence in Syria and other parts of the region, Russia also seeks to challenge the United States' hegemony and assert itself as a significant player in the Middle East.

These external actors' involvement in the Red Sea crisis not only perpetuates violence but also exacerbates regional tensions and rivalries. While each actor pursues its own strategic objectives, their actions often collide, leading to unintended consequences and further complicating diplomatic solutions. The militarization of the Red Sea region and the growing presence of foreign powers heighten the risk of unintended, potentially catastrophic, escalations that could have severe consequences for global security and stability.

To chart a path towards a more peaceful future in the Red Sea region, it is imperative for the international community to recognize the detrimental impact of proxy wars and foreign interventions. Diplomatic efforts must prioritize dialogue and mediation, aiming to de-escalate tensions and foster inclusive negotiations. Addressing the underlying grievances, such as sectarian

divides, political marginalization, and socioeconomic in-
equalities, is crucial for building sustainable peace and
stability.

Furthermore, regional and global powers must reassess their strategies and recognize that military interventions and proxy wars only perpetuate cycles of
violence and suffering. Efforts should be redirected towards comprehensive political solutions that address the
root causes of the conflicts, promote inclusive governance, and prioritize the well-being of the affected populations. Only through such concerted and cooperative
actions can the Red Sea region hope to emerge from the
grip of the crisis and embark on a path of sustainable
development and peace.

D. INVOLVEMENT OF MAJOR GLOBAL POWERS SUCH AS THE US, RUSSIA, IRAN, AND SAUDI ARABIA

The crisis in the Red Sea has captured the attention and involvement of major global powers, each with
their own complex interests and agendas. The United
States, as the world's leading superpower, has a significant stake in maintaining stability and securing the free
flow of goods through international shipping routes.
Its historical presence in the region has engendered a

responsibility to protect its strategic partners and allies in the Middle East, who rely on the Red Sea for trade and security.

The United States' engagement in the Red Sea crisis also stems from its broader regional objectives. With a continued focus on counterterrorism operations and preventing the spread of extremist ideologies, the US recognizes the importance of a stable and secure Red Sea region. The rise of non-state actors such as Al-Qaeda and ISIS in the region has further complicated the security landscape, necessitating US involvement to prevent the expansion of these extremist groups.

Moreover, as energy independence becomes a key priority for the US, safeguarding the transportation of oil and other vital resources through these critical maritime chokepoints is crucial. The Red Sea provides an important passageway for energy supplies between the oil-rich countries of the Persian Gulf and the major consuming markets of Europe and Asia. Any disruption in this corridor would have severe implications for global energy prices and the stability of the global economy.

Russia, ever eager to assert its influence on the global stage, has pursued an active role in the Red Sea. In recent years, it has sought to strengthen its presence in the region through military deployments and the establishment of naval bases. This expansion aligns with Russia's broader geopolitical strategy of expanding its reach across the Middle East and Africa. By cultivating alliances with states such as Sudan and Egypt, Russia aims to gain a foothold in the region and challenge traditional Western dominance.

Russia's involvement in the Red Sea crisis also serves its economic interests. The region is home to vast untapped natural resources and mineral reserves, particularly in countries like Sudan and Eritrea. Access to these resources presents lucrative opportunities for the Russian economy, which has traditionally relied on exports of natural gas and petroleum.

The involvement of Iran, a regional power with its own ambitions, further complicates the Red Sea crisis. Iran has long pursued an agenda of destabilization to challenge its regional rivals, particularly Saudi Arabia and the United States. As a staunch supporter of the Houthi rebels in Yemen, Iran has actively sought to disrupt shipping in the Bab el Mandeb strait, exacerbating tensions in the Red Sea. For Iran, the Red Sea represents an opportunity to project power and disrupt its adversaries' interests, all while advancing its own agenda of regional supremacy.

Iran's engagement in the Red Sea crisis also stems from its desire to break free from US-imposed sanctions and foster economic ties with countries in the region. By establishing alliances with states like Sudan and building infrastructure projects like ports and military facilities, Iran seeks to deepen its influence and strengthen its economic foothold in the Red Sea. This, in turn, allows Iran to circumvent international isolation and access new markets and resources.

Saudi Arabia, a dominant player in the Middle East and a key oil producer, perceives the crisis in the Red Sea as a direct threat to its national security and economic interests. With the Bab el Mandeb strait being a vital transit point for its oil exports, any disruption in this crucial shipping lane has severe implications for the Saudi economy and global energy markets. Saudi Arabia's rivalry with Iran has further escalated tensions in the region, with both countries engaging in naval deployments and supporting proxies to gain an upper hand in the Red Sea.

The involvement of these major global powers has added another layer of complexity to the already intricate Red Sea crisis. Their conflicting interests, geopolitical rivalries, and interventions have not only exacerbated tensions but have also hindered diplomatic efforts to address the issue comprehensively. Furthermore, their engagement underscores the wider strategic and security implications at play, as the Red Sea transforms into a battleground for influence and a focal point for power struggles among major global actors.

Recognizing the potential consequences of the involvement of these major powers in the Red Sea crisis is paramount. Their actions, if not properly managed, could further destabilize the region, escalate ongoing conflicts, and disrupt international trade. Therefore, finding pathways to foster cooperation and dialogue among these powers is essential for ensuring a peaceful resolution and maintaining stability in the Red Sea region. Only by working together can they navigate the complexities and challenges in a manner that upholds both regional and global stability.

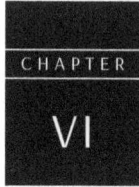

CHOKEPOINTS AND
STRATEGIC IMPORTANCE

The Red Sea region is home to two significant chokepoints that have shaped the course of global trade and international relations – the Suez Canal and the Bab el Mandeb strait. These narrow waterways, connecting the Red Sea to the Mediterranean Sea and the Gulf of Aden respectively, hold immense geopolitical and economic significance, making them vital strategic assets for both states and non-state actors.

The Suez Canal, often referred to as the "Highway to India," is one of the world's busiest maritime trade routes. Opened in 1869, it revolutionized global shipping by providing a direct passage between the Mediterranean and the Red Sea, reducing travel time and costs for vessels traveling between Europe and Asia. Today, the canal accommodates around 10% of global seaborne trade, serving as a key artery for the transportation of goods, including oil, natural gas, raw materials, and manufactured products.

Control over the Suez Canal brings immense economic and political leverage, as it allows the managing state to influence global trade flows, charge transit fees, and shape international maritime policies. Egypt, the country that controls the canal, has historically held a position of significant influence due to its strategic location. The canal's closure or any disruptions would have profound implications for international trade, global supply chains, and energy markets, impacting the economies of multiple nations.

The Suez Canal not only acts as a conduit for trade but also holds military significance. Its strategic location provides a shortcut for naval forces to move between the Mediterranean Sea and the Indian Ocean, increasing flexibility in maritime operations and enabling rapid deployment of naval assets. Throughout history, control of the Suez Canal has been strongly linked to regional conflicts and power struggles. During the 1956 Suez Crisis, the canal became a battlefield of opposing interests, highlighting its strategic value as a military asset.

Similarly, the Bab el Mandeb strait is a vital chokepoint that connects the Red Sea to the Gulf of Aden and ultimately the Indian Ocean. This maritime gateway, located between Yemen and Djibouti, is a crucial transit point for oil tankers traveling from the Persian Gulf region to the West. With approximately 4.8 million barrels of oil passing through each day, the Bab el Mandeb plays a critical role in maintaining global energy security. Any attempts to control or disrupt this chokepoint could lead to major oil price fluctuations, affecting the global economy and energy markets.

Moreover, the Bab el Mandeb strait is not only important for the transportation of oil but also serves as a strategic route for other goods, including manufactured goods, commodities, and military equipment. It is a gateway to the Suez Canal and the Mediterranean, making it a crucial component in global trade networks and maritime security.

The strategic importance of these chokepoints extends beyond their economic significance. They offer military advantages, allowing navies to project power, control access to resources, and protect their national interests. For major powers like the United States, China, Russia, and regional states like Iran, Saudi Arabia, and Egypt, maintaining a presence or influence around these vital maritime arteries directly serves their geopolitical objectives. It is no wonder that these chokepoints have historically been a stage for rivalries, competing interests, and even military confrontations.

Furthermore, non-state actors such as terrorist organizations, pirates, and insurgent groups have recognized the potential benefits of controlling or disrupting these chokepoints. They can exploit the vulnerability of maritime traffic, engage in illegal activities such as smuggling, or even hold ships ransom for economic or political gain. The Red Sea region has witnessed incidents of piracy and attempted interdictions in the past, highlighting the need for robust maritime security measures.

Preserving the security, stability, and freedom of navigation through these chokepoints requires close cooperation and coordination among states and international organizations. Governments must prioritize the safeguarding of these critical waterways and invest in maritime security infrastructure, surveillance capabilities, and response mechanisms. Additionally, collaboration in intelligence-sharing, training, and joint naval patrols can enhance efforts to combat piracy, terrorism, and any threats posed to the uninterrupted flow of global trade.

In conclusion, the Suez Canal and the Bab el Mandeb strait hold immense strategic importance and influence global dynamics in terms of trade, energy security, and military positioning. These chokepoints serve as gateways bridging regions, economies, and geopolitical ambitions. Recognizing their significance, nations and international bodies must work together to ensure the security, stability, and openness of these critical waterways, thereby facilitating global trade, maintaining energy security, and fostering international cooperation.

The continuous monitoring and analysis of the

geopolitical landscape surrounding these chokepoints are crucial to understanding emerging trends that may impact their future significance. Evolving dynamics, such as shifts in regional power, territorial disputes, and infrastructure developments, can reshape the strategic importance of these maritime pathways. For instance, the intensification of conflicts, such as the ongoing civil war in Yemen, threatens the stability and security of the Bab el Mandeb strait, potentially disrupting global trade and energy flows.

Moreover, the rapid growth of China's economic influence and its Belt and Road Initiative (BRI) has placed these chokepoints under increased scrutiny. As China seeks to expand its maritime reach and secure its energy supply lines, its involvement in the Red Sea region, including Djibouti's strategic port, provides Beijing with an avenue to augment its naval capabilities and extend its influence in the Indian Ocean. This trend has raised concerns among other major powers, as they closely monitor China's activities and assess its potential impact on their strategic interests.

Furthermore, the impact of climate change and rising sea levels cannot be ignored when assessing the future of these chokepoints. As global temperatures continue to rise, the potential for melting ice caps and subsequent sea-level rise could impact the security and viability of these vital passages. Coastal areas surrounding the Suez Canal and the Bab el Mandeb strait may face increased vulnerability to flooding and erosion, necessitating long-term adaptation strategies to protect crucial infra-structure and ensure uninterrupted navigation.

To navigate the complex geopolitical realities and risks associated with these chokepoints, regional and international cooperation is fundamental. Collaboration between littoral states, adjacent powers, and interna-tional organizations is crucial to address challenges such as piracy, terrorism, and illicit activities. Platforms like the Red Sea Forum, which brings together countries in the region to discuss shared concerns and promote dialogue, serve as valuable mechanisms for enhancing coordination and building trust.

In conclusion, the strategic importance of the Suez Canal and the Bab el Mandeb strait extends beyond their economic significance. These chokepoints are pivotal to global trade, energy security, and military position-ing. Monitoring geopolitical developments, understand-ing emerging trends, and fostering cooperation among stakeholders are vital to safeguarding the security, sta-bility, and openness of these critical waterways. As the world evolves, so too must strategies and policies re-garding the Red Sea region's chokepoints, ensuring their enduring significance for generations to come.

A. SIGNIFICANCE OF THE SUEZ CANAL AND THE BAB EL MANDEB AS CHOKE-POINTS IN THE RED SEA

The Suez Canal and the Bab el Mandeb are two vital chokepoints within the Red Sea region that hold immense significance in global maritime trade and security. These strategic waterways serve as major arteries for the movement of goods, particularly crude oil, between the Mediterranean Sea, Red Sea, and Indian Ocean. This chapter examines the significance of the Suez Canal and the Bab el Mandeb and their role as essential chokepoints in the Red Sea.

The Suez Canal, located in Egypt, is a 193 km long artificial waterway connecting the Mediterranean Sea to the Red Sea. Its construction, spearheaded by French diplomat Ferdinand de Lesseps and completed in 1869, revolutionized global trade by providing a direct shipping route between Europe and Asia. Prior to the canal's existence, vessels had to undertake a time-consuming and perilous journey around the Cape of Good Hope in southern Africa. The creation of this shortcut reduced travel time and expenses significantly, giving a powerful impetus to trade and opening up new opportunities for economic growth and development.

The economic impact of the Suez Canal cannot be overstated. Today, it is one of the busiest shipping lanes globally, handling approximately 10% of global maritime trade, including significant volumes of oil, natural gas, and manufactured goods. Every year, thousands of vessels pass through its locks, allowing for the transportation of goods between East and West, linking major trade hubs like China, Europe, and the Middle East. This efficient route enables quicker delivery of goods, lowers shipping costs, and promotes global economic integration.

In terms of oil transport, the Suez Canal plays a significant role in connecting major oil-producing regions in the Middle East, such as Saudi Arabia, Iraq, and Iran, to global markets. A substantial fraction of the world's oil supply traverses this crucial waterway, reaching Europe, Asia, and even the United States. Any closure or disruption of the Suez Canal would force ships to take much longer alternative routes, such as around the Cape of Good Hope or through the Strait of Hormuz, raising transportation costs and potentially causing delays in the supply chain. Moreover, any disruption in the Suez Canal could have implications for global energy security and lead to hikes in oil prices, affecting both businesses and consumers worldwide.

Similarly, the Bab el Mandeb strait, located at the southern end of the Red Sea, acts as a chokepoint connecting the Red Sea to the Gulf of Aden and the Arabian Sea. It is an essential gateway for maritime traffic between the Mediterranean and Indian Ocean, offering a crucial link between Europe, Africa, and Asia. Ships passing through the Bab el Mandeb strait not only transport oil but also a wide array of goods, including manufactured products, raw materials, and agricultural commodities. Being in close proximity to major oil producers like Saudi Arabia and others in the Arabian Peninsula, the Bab el Mandeb strait assumes strategic importance in ensuring the smooth and uninterrupted flow of oil to global markets.

Controlling the Suez Canal and the Bab el Mandeb has historically been of utmost importance for both regional powers and global players. These chokepoints offer significant economic advantages, as they allow countries to exert influence over global trade routes and ensure their interests are protected. Throughout history, various nations have sought to project power and secure their economic and strategic interests by establishing a presence in the Red Sea region. For instance, in the era of colonialism, European powers competed for dominance in the Red Sea, recognizing the immense commercial and strategic potential of these chokepoints.

Moreover, the Red Sea region has also witnessed its fair share of conflicts and instabilities. Piracy, particularly off the coast of Somalia, has posed a significant threat to shipping in the region. Vessels passing through the Bab el Mandeb strait have been targeted by pirates seeking ransom or plundering cargo. These pirate activities not only disrupt maritime trade but also pose risks to the safety of seafarers. Regional conflicts, like the ongoing civil war in Yemen, have also impacted the security of the Red Sea region. The Bab el Mandeb strait, in particular, has been a site of military confrontations and naval blockades, further underscoring the vulnerability of these crucial waterways to geopolitical tensions and conflicts.

Given the importance of these chokepoints, any instability or insecurity in the Red Sea region poses a direct threat to global maritime trade, energy security, and the stability of the international economy. The vulnerability of the Suez Canal and the Bab el Mandeb to piracy, terrorism, regional conflicts, or political disputes highlights the need for international cooperation in ensuring the safety and security of these critical waterways. Increased counter-piracy operations, maritime patrols, and cooperation between regional and international naval forces have been crucial in mitigating risks and maintaining the free flow of goods through these vital shipping routes.

Furthermore, environmental challenges also impact the Red Sea region and its chokepoints. Climate change, rising sea levels, and coral bleaching pose risks to the delicate ecosystem of the Red Sea. These changes not only affect marine life but can also have economic consequences by impeding navigation and causing potential damage to infrastructure such as ports and terminals. The importance of sustainable practices and environmental protection in the Red Sea cannot be overlooked, as maintaining the ecological health of the region is crucial for the long-term viability of the Suez Canal and the Bab el Mandeb.

In conclusion, the significance of the Suez Canal and

the Bab el Mandeb as chokepoints in the Red Sea cannot be understated. They are essential conduits for international trade and energy transportation, connecting major economic regions and facilitating the movement of goods. The creation of the Suez Canal transformed global trade dynamics, providing a more direct and efficient route between Europe and Asia. Likewise, the Bab el Mandeb strait serves as a crucial gateway for maritime traffic between the Mediterranean and Indian Ocean. Understanding the importance of these chokepoints and the potential risks they face is essential for maintaining global trade stability, promoting energy security, and ensuring the uninterrupted flow of goods through these vital waterways. Additionally, mitigating environmental challenges and fostering sustainable practices in the region are crucial for the long-term viability and resilience of these chokepoints in the face of changing environmental conditions.

B. DESIRABILITY OF CONTROLLING THESE CHOKEPOINTS FOR STATES AND NON-STATE ACTORS

The strategic importance of control over chokepoints, such as the Suez Canal, the Bab el Mandeb strait, and the Strait of Hormuz, cannot be understated. These narrow passages play a critical role in facilitating global trade and shaping geopolitical dynamics, and both states and non-state actors recognize the immense benefits that come from holding such strategic maritime territories.

For states, controlling chokepoints offers a range of advantages that extend beyond mere commercial interests. Firstly, it provides significant influence over international trade and the flow of goods. More than 90% of global trade is transported by sea, and thus, control over these vital shipping lanes allows states to exert control over global supply chains, impacting economies and shaping the balance of power on the international stage. By dominating chokepoints, states can strategically dictate and influence the movement of goods, giving them a position of advantage in commercial negotiations and geopolitical discussions.

Moreover, chokepoints offer possibilities for revenue generation. States that control these strategic maritime passages can impose tariffs, fees, or tolls on vessels passing through, thereby generating substantial income. This revenue can be utilized to boost a nation's economy, invest in infrastructure development, or even fund military capabilities, further augmenting its overall power and influence.

In addition to economic benefits, control over chokepoints provides states with a significant military advantage. These narrow passages serve as logistical and strategic lifelines, enabling the rapid deployment of naval forces to different regions. By dominating chokepoints, states can effectively project their military power, control access to critical resources, and shape the outcomes of conflicts in their favor. Furthermore, chokepoints offer ideal locations for the establishment of naval bases and military facilities, allowing states to enhance their security and extend their reach in the broader maritime domain.

Non-state actors, such as insurgent groups, terrorists, pirates, and criminal organizations, also recognize the desirability of controlling chokepoints. For these actors, control of strategic maritime passages provides significant leverage and opportunities for illicit activities. Insurgent groups may seek control to smuggle arms or supplies, allowing them to sustain their operations or exert influence over the region. Terrorist organizations, in particular, can exploit chokepoints as transit points for the movement of fighters, weapons, and illicit funds, making it challenging for security forces to monitor and disrupt their activities. Pirates, on the other hand, take advantage of the vulnerability of these narrow passages to hijack vessels and extort ransom, capitalizing on the fear and disruption they cause.

The implications of controlling chokepoints are not limited to economic and security considerations alone. Environmental concerns also come into play, especially in areas with delicate ecosystems and marine habitats. Accidental oil spills or intentional sabotages can result in catastrophic damage to these fragile environments, affecting biodiversity, fisheries, and the livelihoods of local communities. Therefore, the responsibility of ensuring the safety and protection of these strategic maritime passages extends beyond national interests to international cooperation and the commitment to environmental sustainability.

In recent years, both state and non-state actors have taken advantage of the strategic importance of chokepoints, particularly in the Red Sea region. The rise of piracy off the coast of Somalia, the ongoing conflicts in Yemen and Syria, and tensions between Iran and the international community over the Strait of Hormuz have highlighted the vulnerabilities of these critical waterways. These incidents have not only caused significant economic losses for the shipping industry but have also created an urgent need for increased security measures and international cooperation to ensure the safe passage of vessels and uninterrupted global trade.

In response to these challenges, global powers have recognized the importance of maintaining stability and security in these chokepoints. International naval missions, such as the Combined Maritime Forces and the European Union Naval Force, have been established to combat piracy, enhance maritime security, and protect shipping lanes in critical regions. Additionally, there have been efforts to develop more comprehensive legal frameworks and cooperative agreements to deter and suppress criminal activities in these areas.

However, the complexity and dynamic nature of chokepoint control in the current geopolitical landscape necessitate continuous monitoring and adaptation. As international order evolves, new actors emerge, and technological advancements influence maritime operations, it becomes crucial for global powers to anticipate and address potential challenges in controlling and securing chokepoints. Ensuring the freedom of navigation and safeguarding global trade requires sustained international cooperation, shared security responsibilities, and robust maritime strategies that encompass diplomacy, deterrence, and effective enforcement.

In conclusion, the desirability of controlling chokepoints in the Red Sea region, such as the Suez Canal, the Bab el Mandeb strait, and the Strait of Hormuz, extends beyond commercial interests. The ability to influence trade, generate revenue, exert military leverage, engage in illicit activities, and protect the environment makes these maritime passages highly sought after. As such, it is imperative for international powers to recognize the strategic importance of maintaining stability and security in these chokepoints, collaborating to safeguard global trade, ensure the free movement of goods, and counter the threats posed by both state and non-state actors. The world's reliance on maritime trade necessitates a comprehensive approach, integrating economic, security, and environmental considerations, in order to effectively address the challenges associated with chokepoint control and ensure a stable and prosperous global order.

C. INFLUENCE OF CHOKEPOINT CONTROL ON INTERNATIONAL POLITICS AND POWER DYNAMICS

The control of chokepoints in international waterways, such as the Red Sea's Bab el Mandeb strait and the Suez Canal, has profound implications for global politics, economics, and security dynamics. These critical maritime passages act as strategic arteries through which a substantial volume of global trade flows, making them highly coveted assets for nations seeking to maintain and expand their influence on the world stage.

The repercussions of chokepoint control are far-reaching and leave an indelible imprint on international politics. Nations that assert control over these passages possess the authority to regulate and restrict the movement of vessels, granting them leverage over other countries dependent on these routes for trade. This power can be wielded through various means, such as imposing transit fees, implementing security measures, or even denying passage to certain vessels. Such control provides a platform for geopolitical maneuvering, allowing states to project their power, secure alliances, and assert dominance in the region.

The strategic value of chokepoints becomes particularly evident when examining the Red Sea region. The Bab el Mandeb strait, connecting the Red Sea to the Gulf of Aden and the Arabian Sea, serves as a critical link in the global maritime trade network. Not only does it facilitate the transport of goods, but it also acts as a transit route for energy resources, including oil and liquefied natural gas. Thus, the ability to control this chokepoint grants nations the capacity to disrupt global energy supplies, exert influence over the energy-dependent economies of various countries, and manipulate the balance of power.

The control of chokepoints also plays a vital role in naval power projection. Nations with robust naval capabilities can leverage their control of these passages to establish strategic bases, monitor the activities of rival powers, and safeguard their own interests. For instance, a dominant control over the Bab el Mandeb strait would enable a country to monitor and potentially interdict naval assets passing through, thereby enhancing its regional presence and potentially deterring adversaries. This level of control allows countries to effectively exert their military influence and shape the balance of power in maritime regions.

Moreover, chokepoint control significantly affects regional security dynamics by influencing alliances and partnerships. States with shared interests in controlling a chokepoint may form cooperative arrangements to ensure the stability and security of the passage. These alliances often involve multiple actors, including regional powers, global powers, and multinational organizations. However, rival nations may compete for control, leading to the formation of alliances that heighten tensions and escalate conflicts. The struggle for chokepoint control in the Red Sea region exemplifies this dynamic, with various countries aligning themselves based on their economic, military, and strategic objectives.

In addition to its impact on security and geopolitics, chokepoint control carries significant economic implications. Nations that control critical passages often generate substantial revenue from tolls and fees imposed on vessels passing through. These financial resources can be utilized to bolster their economies, invest in infrastructure development, and enhance military capabilities, further consolidating their power on a global scale. Furthermore, chokepoint control also influences trade patterns and the cost of goods, as disruptions or increased costs resulting from a change in control can reverberate throughout the global economy.

Beyond its immediate strategic and economic implications, chokepoint control holds broader geopolitical significance. It raises fundamental questions about the principles and norms governing international maritime governance. The freedom of navigation and the right of innocent passage, principles enshrined in the United Nations Convention on the Law of the Sea, may face challenges or undermine by the actions of states seeking to assert control over these critical passages. The tension between the interests of navigating states and the sovereign claims of coastal states further complicate the issue, requiring delicate diplomacy and negotiation to strike a balance between national and international interests.

In conclusion, the control of chokepoints, such as the Bab el Mandeb strait, profoundly impacts global politics, economics, and security dynamics. It provides countries with opportunities to exert influence, shape alliances, project military power, and control vital trade routes. As such, chokepoint control is a crucial aspect of contemporary geopolitics, deserving careful consideration and analysis to understand global power structures and their impact on international relations. The intricate interplay between military, economic, and diplomatic factors in the struggle for chokepoint control underscores the complexity of these issues and the strategic calculations made by states in the pursuit of their national interests.

INTERSTATE RIVALRY AND COMPETITION

Interstate Rivalry and Competition in the Red Sea Region: A Complex Geopolitical Landscape

The Red Sea region stands as a cauldron of intense interstate rivalry and competition, captivating the attention of major regional and global powers. This strategic area has witnessed a complex web of political maneuvering, conflicts, and conflicting agendas, which have far-reaching implications for regional stability and international security.

GEW REPORTS & ANALYSES TEAM

Iran, as a major regional power, endeavors to expand its influence in the Red Sea region as part of its broader strategy to establish itself as a regional hegemon. With its alliances and support for Shia communities and movements, Iran has effectively carved out a sphere of influence stretching from Lebanon to Yemen, posing a direct challenge to Saudi Arabia's security and interests. Through its support for the Houthi rebels in Yemen, Iran has created a formidable proxy force, which has sustained a prolonged conflict presenting a significant threat to Saudi Arabia's southern border.

The Saudi-Iranian rivalry, rooted in religious and sectarian differences, significantly shapes the dynamics of the region. As the birthplace of Islam and home to its two holiest cities, Mecca and Medina, Saudi Arabia presents itself as the guardian of Sunni Islam. Conversely, Iran represents the Shia sect and sees itself as a champion for the marginalized Shia communities in the region. This religious and sectarian tension has fueled deep divisions and intensified the competition for dominance, hindering the prospects for peaceful coexistence and regional stability.

Egypt, with its historical ties and strategic interests in the Red Sea region, also seeks to maintain and secure its influence. As the most populous country in the Arab world and a major player in regional affairs, Egypt plays a central role in shaping the dynamics of the region. It has historically used its military and diplomatic power to project its interests, intervening in conflicts and supporting various factions and governments. Egypt perceives itself as a stable anchor of regional power, upholding its role as a guardian of Arab nationalism and seeking to counter threats to its national security, including terrorism and the spread of extremism.

The competition among these regional powers is not limited to ideological or religious factors. Control over the Red Sea region has a significant impact on global energy supplies and maritime trade. The maritime chokepoints of the Bab el Mandeb and the Suez Canal are vital arteries for international commerce, facilitating the transportation of goods, energy resources, and military assets. Ensuring the safety and security of these crucial waterways is of paramount importance, as any escalation in tensions or disruptions could have severe consequences, including piracy, attacks on commercial ships, and disruptions to global trade.

The complexity of interstate rivalry in the Red Sea region is further compounded by the involvement of major global powers. The United States, Russia, and China, recognizing the strategic significance of the region, have also become entangled in the competition for influence. These global actors, driven by their own strategic interests, often align with different factions or governments, escalating the intensity of the rivalry. As they seek to secure their interests, these powers have increased their military presence, conducted naval patrols, and provided financial and military support to regional allies, further complicating the delicate balance of power.

To address the multifaceted challenges posed by interstate rivalry in the Red Sea region, a comprehensive and cooperative approach is crucial. Regional powers must prioritize stability and regional security above narrow national interests, fostering dialogue and cooperation while deterring escalation. Emphasizing confidence-building measures, diplomatic initiatives, and mediation can create a platform for resolving disputes and deescalating tensions.

International actors, including global powers and organizations, have a responsibility to support the search for peaceful solutions. Through multilateral efforts and partnerships, the international community can bolster regional stability, facilitate dialogue, and ensure the respect for international law. Engaging in comprehensive regional diplomacy that acknowledges historical tensions and grievances, as well as socioeconomic and political factors, is vital in alleviating the root causes of the conflicts and forging sustainable peace.

Moreover, addressing the socioeconomic aspects of interstate rivalry is essential for fostering stability in the Red Sea region. Promoting economic development, reducing poverty, and addressing socio-political grievances are critical steps towards creating an environment conducive to peace. By supporting inclusive governance, encouraging regional integration, and investing in education and infrastructure, the international community can help diminish the sources of instability and contribute to long-lasting peace in the region.

In conclusion, the interstate rivalry and competition in the Red Sea region form a complex geopolitical landscape with far-reaching implications for regional stability and international security. Iran, Saudi Arabia, and Egypt, along with other regional and global powers, engage in a multifaceted competition for dominance fueled by ideological, religious, and strategic differences. Resolving the challenges of this rivalry demands a cooperative and comprehensive approach that prioritizes stability, fosters dialogue, and addresses the socioeconomic factors underlying the conflicts. Only through inclusive regional diplomacy, supported by global actors committed to peace, can the Red Sea region realize its potential as a crucible of prosperity, cooperation, and security.

A. INTENSE RIVALRY AMONG REGIONAL POWERS LIKE IRAN, SAUDI ARABIA, AND EGYPT

Intense rivalry among regional powers like Iran, Saudi Arabia, and Egypt is a significant factor contributing to the complicated geopolitical situation in the Red Sea region. These three countries, with their respective agendas, vie for influence and power in a region that holds immense economic and strategic value.

The sectarian divide between Shia-majority Iran and

Sunni-majority Saudi Arabia plays a crucial role in fueling this rivalry. Both countries view themselves as leaders of their respective sects, making the competition for influence among the Muslim population even more pronounced. This rivalry has spilled over into various conflicts across the Middle East, with each country supporting opposing factions, exacerbating tensions in the Red Sea region.

Iran, seeking to expand its influence, has found allies in countries like Yemen and Sudan. In Yemen, Iran backs the Houthi rebels, providing them with financial and military support. The Houthi rebellion against the internationally recognized government, supported by the Saudi-led coalition, has turned Yemen into a battleground for regional powers. Iran's involvement in Yemen aims to challenge Saudi Arabia's dominance and extend its reach through its support for Houthi-led forces.

Sudan, another country where Iran seeks influence, allows the Iranian navy to use its Red Sea naval base in Port Sudan. This alliance gives Iran a foothold in the region, allowing it to project power and potentially disrupt maritime routes. Furthermore, Iran has been cultivating relationships with Eritrea and Somalia, expanding its reach across the Horn of Africa. These efforts enable Iran to establish a network of influence, challenging Saudi Arabia's traditionally dominant position in the region.

Saudi Arabia, on the other hand, seeks to maintain its dominance in the region and protect its interests. It has forged closer ties with Egypt, a significant regional power and the most populous Arab country, to counter Iran's influence. Egypt, with its strategic location, strong military capabilities, and historical rivalry with Iran stemming from the Islamic revolution in 1979, has become an important ally in the Saudi-led coalition. The alliance between Saudi Arabia and Egypt aims to counter Iranian expansionist ambitions and ensure regional stability. Saudi Arabia also provides Egypt with significant financial aid, which strengthens their partnership.

The competition between these regional powers extends beyond ideological differences. Control over strategic areas within the Red Sea, such as ports and maritime routes, is also a key factor. These powers seek dominance over these crucial points to secure their trade routes, influence regional affairs, and project power beyond their borders.

For instance, in addition to the Bab el-Mandeb Strait, the Red Sea encompasses other important chokepoints and vital maritime routes. The Suez Canal in Egypt, linking the Mediterranean Sea to the Red Sea, is a critical passage for global trade, with approximately 10% of the world's seaborne oil trade passing through it. Maintaining control and ensuring the security of these routes is a shared interest among regional powers.

Furthermore, the Red Sea region holds substantial offshore oil and gas reserves, attracting international attention and investment. Countries like Saudi Arabia and Iran, both major oil producers, have a vested interest in securing access to these resources, adding an economic dimension to their rivalry. The proximity of the Red Sea to key global markets and the importance of its shipping routes make it a strategic prize coveted by these powers.

In this dynamic arena, outside forces, such as the United States, Russia, and China, have also entered into the fray, seeking to advance their own interests and potentially exacerbating these rivalries. The United States, for instance, has steadily increased its military presence in the region, utilizing its military bases in Djibouti and backing the Saudi-led coalition in Yemen to counter Iranian influence. Russia, on the other hand, has been engaging in diplomatic maneuvers and military agreements, such as the establishment of a naval logistics base in Sudan, in an attempt to expand its influence in the region. China, a significant investor in the Red Sea region, has been actively involved in infrastructure development projects, seeking access to resources and establishing economic partnerships. Their involvement adds another layer of complexity to an already volatile situation.

The complex web of alliances, conflicting agendas, and interests adds significant depth to the geopolitical landscape of the Red Sea region. Finding a path towards stability will require diplomatic engagement and cooperation among these powers, as well as broader international efforts to mitigate tensions and promote regional stability. Failure to address and manage these rivalries risks further escalation of conflicts, destabilization of the region, and potential disruptions to global trade and security.

B. STRUGGLE FOR INFLUENCE AND FORMATION OF ALLIANCES TO ACHIEVE GEOPOLITICAL GOALS

Beneath the turbulent surface of the Red Sea lies a complex web of geopolitical interests, rivalries, and alliances that continue to shape the region's trajectory. As states vie for influence, borders are blurred, power dynamics shift, and the implications reverberate far beyond the shores of this strategic waterway.

Amidst this tumultuous landscape, Iran's quest for regional dominance remains a primary driving force. Capitalizing on its revolutionary ideology and the power vacuum in the region, Iran has been methodically expanding its influence through various means. One prominent example is its support for the Houthi rebels in Yemen. By providing arms, funding, and training, Iran seeks to harness the Houthi movement as a means to counter its arch-rival, Saudi Arabia, and assert its dominance in the region. Through its support of the Houthi rebels, Iran aims to establish a foothold on the Arabian Peninsula, gaining access to the Red Sea and potentially controlling key maritime routes. Furthermore,

Iran's support for proxy groups in Yemen highlights its broader strategy of utilizing non-state actors to further its regional objectives.

The Iranian-Saudi power struggle animates much of the Red Sea's geopolitical dynamics. Saudi Arabia, traditionally regarded as the leading power in the region, perceives Iran's ascendancy as a direct threat to its own primacy. Saudi Arabia's concerns stem not only from Iran's military capabilities but also from its ideological challenge to the Sunni-dominated Gulf monarchies. In response, Saudi Arabia has formed the Arab Coalition, a unified front supported by various Gulf Cooperation Council (GCC) states, including the United Arab Emirates and Bahrain. This alliance aims to thwart Iran's ambitions and restore stability in Yemen by supporting the internationally recognized government. By intervening militarily, the Arab Coalition seeks to prevent Yemen from becoming a launching pad for Iran's expansionist agenda. Yet, beyond Yemen, the Arab Coalition also serves as a bulwark against Iran's regional ambitions, safeguarding strategic interests in the Red Sea and countering the influence of Shia ideology.

Egypt, a historic regional power and guardian of the Suez Canal, has its own set of geopolitical interests in the Red Sea. With a history of strained relations with both Iran and Saudi Arabia, Egypt toes a delicate line, cautiously preserving its standing as a peace broker and mediator. Concerned with its own internal stability and the threat of Islamist extremism, Egypt aligns itself with Saudi Arabia's stance against Iran's expansionist agenda. Additionally, Egypt views the Red Sea as a vital economic lifeline, as it relies heavily on maritime trade passing through the Suez Canal. Egypt seeks to promote stability, prevent the rise of extremist factions, and safeguard its own corridors of influence in a region plagued by volatility.

The struggle for influence in the Red Sea region is not solely confined to state actors. Non-state actors, particularly extremist groups, add another layer of complexity to the geopolitical landscape. Al-Qaeda in the Arabian Peninsula (AQAP) and the Islamic State (ISIS), seeing an opportunity in the region's instability, exploit power vacuums, religious divides, and local grievances to expand their influence. These extremist groups pose not only a direct threat to regional stability and security but also complicate efforts by state actors to achieve their geopolitical goals. The ascendancy of AQAP and ISIS in the Red Sea region not only exacerbates sectarian tensions but also poses a challenge to established power structures, as these groups attempt to carve out their own spheres of influence.

As power struggles and rivalries intensify, alliances in the Red Sea region have become crucial instruments for advancing geopolitical objectives. These alliances are forged based on shared interests, ideological alignment, and regional dynamics. For instance, Saudi Arabia's alliance with the United Arab Emirates and Bahrain within the GCC, in addition to its partnership with Egypt, forms a robust coalition against Iran's influence. The GCC countries, facing the Iranian threat and fears of domino effects from the Arab Spring, have collectively prioritized stability and the preservation of the regional status quo.

Moreover, alliances within the region extend beyond states and include international actors. The United States maintains close ties with Saudi Arabia and views the Red Sea as a critical arena for countering Iran's influence and ensuring the stability of the global energy market. With its massive naval presence and military capabilities in the Red Sea, the U.S. seeks to deter potential threats, supporting its allies and shaping the regional balance of power. Russia, on the other hand, seeks to expand its presence and leverage its influence in the region, particularly through its support for the Bashar al-Assad regime in Syria. Russia's military involvement in Syria allows it to project power beyond its traditional sphere of influence and challenge the U.S. dominance in the region. By backing Assad, Russia indirectly supports Iran's regional aspirations, potentially enhancing its own leverage in the Red Sea and augmenting its presence in the Eastern Mediterranean.

These external alliances further shape the geopolitical dynamics of the Red Sea region. With different interests and actors competing for influence, the region becomes a convoluted arena of strategic maneuvering and geopolitical calculations. The outcome of these power struggles will not only determine the fate of the Red Sea region but will also have profound long-term implications for regional stability, global security, and the intricate web of alliances that govern the modern geopolitical landscape.

C. CONSEQUENCES OF INTERSTATE RIVALRY ON MARINE SAFETY AND STABILITY IN THE RED SEA

The Red Sea region has become a hotbed of interstate rivalry, with various regional powers vying for influence and dominance. Unfortunately, this intense competition among states has severe consequences for marine safety and stability in the Red Sea, which, when examined more closely, reveal a web of interconnected challenges and complexities.

One of the immediate repercussions of interstate rivalry is the increased risk of maritime incidents and accidents. As rival states try to assert control over key strategic positions and chokepoints, such as the Bab el Mandeb strait, tensions escalate, and the likelihood of naval skirmishes or confrontations rises. This, in turn, puts commercial shipping at risk, as vessels passing through these volatile waters can become inadvertent targets or caught in the crossfire. The potential consequences of such incidents extend beyond immediate safety concerns, as disruptions to maritime trade can lead to economic losses for both regional and global actors.

Interstate rivalries also contribute to a lack of co-operation and coordination in ensuring maritime security. Instead of collaborating to combat common threats such as piracy or terrorism, rival states often prioritize their own interests and security concerns, neglecting the broader goal of maintaining stability in the Red Sea region. This fragmented approach to maritime security hampers effective countermeasures, leaving commercial ships vulnerable to attacks and hindering efforts to combat illicit activities. Furthermore, the lack of collaboration paves the way for the proliferation of criminal networks that exploit the resulting security gaps, exacerbating the challenges faced by regional actors.

Moreover, the competition among states has a negative impact on regional diplomacy and conflict resolution. The focus on outdoing one another often prevents meaningful dialogue and negotiation, perpetuating cycles of violence and instability. Key issues related to maritime security, such as disputed boundaries or resource exploitation, are often weaponized as tools for interstate rivalry. This further complicates efforts to establish peaceful resolutions and leaves maritime safety at stake. In the absence of diplomatic progress, the risk of conflicts spiraling out of control and spilling over into international waters continues to loom large.

In addition to the immediate consequences, long-term ramifications of interstate rivalry on marine safety and stability in the Red Sea are worrisome. The lack of trust and cooperation among rival states erodes the foundation for regional collaboration, making it challenging to establish effective mechanisms for crisis management and conflict resolution. Without strong regional institutions and agreements, the potential for future conflicts and disruptions to maritime trade remains high. A collective effort to build trust and foster cooperation is therefore crucial for reducing tensions and creating a conducive environment for addressing shared challenges.

Furthermore, the adverse effects of interstate rivalry on marine safety extend to environmental concerns. Increased militarization and conflict in the Red Sea region can lead to unintended ecological consequences. Oil spills, damage to delicate ecosystems, and disruption of migration patterns could occur due to the heightened presence of military vessels and the potential for conflict-induced accidents. The degradation of the marine environment not only negatively impacts marine biodiversity but also affects the livelihoods of coastal communities that rely on fishing and tourism. Protecting the delicate balance of the Red Sea's ecosystem must be a priority for preventing irreversible damage to this unique and ecologically significant region.

The consequences of interstate rivalry also have significant implications for the economies of the countries in the Red Sea region. Persistent instability and insecurity deter foreign investments, hampering economic growth and development. Additionally, the rising costs of maritime insurance and security measures, necessary to mitigate the risks associated with interstate rivalry, burden businesses operating in the Red Sea, leading to higher prices for goods and services. The resulting economic strain further perpetuates social and political discontent, potentially increasing the likelihood of further conflict and instability.

Lastly, interstate rivalries in the Red Sea region have broader implications for global trade and security. The Red Sea is a vital maritime corridor connecting East and West, with a significant portion of global trade passing through its waters. Any disruption or instability in the region can have a ripple effect on global supply chains, causing economic disarray and affecting multiple industries. The dependence of global trade on the stability and safety of the Red Sea underscores the importance of addressing interstate rivalries and working towards lasting solutions that promote peace and cooperation. A stable and secure Red Sea not only benefits regional actors but also contributes to the overall resilience and stability of the global maritime trading system.

In conclusion, the consequences of interstate rivalry on marine safety and stability in the Red Sea are profound and multifaceted. These rivalries contribute to increased risks for commercial shipping, undermine regional cooperation, hinder conflict resolution efforts, harm the environment, impede economic growth, and have wider implications for global trade. Given the interconnectedness of the modern world, it is imperative that the international community recognizes the dangers posed by interstate rivalries in the Red Sea and works towards fostering cooperation, stability, and sustainable development to ensure the safety of maritime activities in the region and beyond. Finding common ground and establishing mechanisms for dialogue and collaboration is essential for addressing the complex and intercon-nected challenges in the Red Sea region, and ultimately achieving a more secure and stable maritime environ-ment that benefits all stakeholders.

COMPLEX GEOPOLITICAL SITUATION

The Red Sea region is mired in a complex web of political, social, and economic dynamics that contribute to the current crisis. This chapter delves into the intricate layers of the region, exploring the multiple factors that exacerbate tensions and hinder diplomatic resolutions.

A. Complications arising from ethnic and religious divides in the Red Sea region The Red Sea region is a melting pot of diverse ethnicities and religious groups, each with their own aspirations, grievances, and sense of identity. The Arab population represents a significant ethnic group in many countries along the Red Sea, such as Saudi Arabia, Egypt, and Sudan, holding varying degrees of political power and influence. In addition to Arabs, other ethnic groups within the region include the Beja, Afar, Nubians, and various tribes, each with their own historical heritage and cultural distinctiveness.

Religious divisions further complicate the socio-political fabric of the Red Sea region. Islam prevails as the predominant religion, with Sunni Muslims constituting the largest religious group. However, within this broad category, there exists a tapestry of diverse strands and interpretations. Additionally, there are significant Shiite Muslim populations, particularly in countries such as Yemen, Bahrain, and Iran. These Shiite communities, while relatively smaller in numbers, hold unique religious and cultural practices that have shaped their identities within the broader Muslim world.

The region is also home to various Christian denominations, including Coptic Christians in Egypt and Ethiopian Orthodox Christians in Ethiopia and Eritrea, who contribute to the rich religious diversity of the Red Sea region. Furthermore, smaller communities of Jews, Baha'is, and Hindus are also present, adding to the vibrant tapestry of faiths in the region.

These ethnic and religious divides often intertwine, fueling internal conflicts and providing opportunities for external actors to exploit existing fault lines. Dissatisfaction stemming from marginalized ethnic or religious groups, with a lack of representation and power-sharing agreements, can ignite tensions and result in protracted conflicts. Historical grievances arising from past

conflicts, religious disputes, and socioeconomic disparities further contribute to these divisions.

B. Impact of sectarian strife on diplomatic attempts
to resolve the crisis Sectarianism, particularly between
Sunni and Shiite factions, has played a significant role
in shaping conflicts in the Red Sea region. The historical divide between these two major branches of Islam
has fueled intense rivalries, proxy wars, and political
power struggles, further complicating the geopolitical
landscape.

The ongoing rivalry between Saudi Arabia and Iran
represents one of the most prominent examples of sectarian tensions in the region. This rivalry extends beyond mere political competition as both countries strive
for regional influence and seek to assert themselves as
leaders of the Muslim world. Their ideological and religious differences further inflame the conflict, creating a
geopolitical battleground where their proxies and allies
engage in proxy conflicts.

Moreover, sectarian strife within countries such as
Yemen and Bahrain has also hindered diplomatic resolutions. In Yemen, the Houthi rebels, who belong to the
Zaidi Shiite sect, have been engaged in a protracted conflict against the Yemeni government led by President
Abdrabbuh Mansur Hadi, who is predominantly Sunni.
The deep-rooted sectarian divisions and historical grievances have complicated efforts to find a peaceful solution, especially as external powers, such as Iran and

Saudi Arabia, back different sides based on sectarian allegiance.

In Bahrain, the Sunni royal family faces opposition from Shiite-led political groups. These tensions, rooted in long-standing religious and political disparities, have sparked protests and instability, making diplomatic resolutions a challenging feat. The delicate balance in countries like Bahrain, where a religious majority holds a political minority status, further exacerbates sectarian rifts and hampers effective conflict resolution.

C. The role of outside forces forming alliances based on religious principles External powers have strategically leveraged religious affiliations and formed alliances based on religious principles to advance their interests in the Red Sea region. Iran, as a predominantly Shiite power, has sought to support Shiite factions across the region, including the Houthi rebels in Yemen and Shiite opposition groups in Bahrain. By providing political, financial, and military support to these groups, Iran aims to expand its influence and counter the influence of its rivals, particularly Saudi Arabia.

On the other hand, Saudi Arabia, as the custodian of the Muslim holy sites in Mecca and Medina and a predominantly Sunni power, has sought to counter Iran's growing influence. Saudi Arabia supports Sunni-led governments, particularly in Yemen and Egypt, to combat what they perceive as a Shiite threat. This dynamic has further polarized the Red Sea region along religious lines, fueling animosity and making diplomatic resolutions increasingly challenging.

Meanwhile, regional and international powers have also sought to exploit these sectarian and religious divides for their own strategic interests. Countries like Turkey, Egypt, Qatar, and the United Arab Emirates (UAE) have backed different factions within the Red Sea region, aligning themselves with specific religious or ethnic groups to gain influence and control over vital strategic assets, such as ports and trade routes.

This utilization of religious affiliations and alliances based on sectarian identity amplifies existing divisions and contributes to the destabilization of the Red Sea region. As external powers vie for influence and manipulate sectarian tensions, rivalries deepen, and resolutions to the crisis become more elusive.

In conclusion, the complex geopolitical situation in the Red Sea region arises from a combination of ethnic and religious divides, sectarian strife, and the involvement of external forces. These factors make finding a resolution even more challenging, as they perpetuate rivalries, fuel conflicts, and hinder diplomatic efforts. Any comprehensive solution to the crisis must consider the intricate dynamics at play, addressing ethnic and religious grievances, fostering inclusive governance, and engaging in dialogue to achieve sustainable peace and stability in the Red Sea region.

A. COMPLICATIONS ARISING FROM ETHNIC AND RELIGIOUS DIVIDES IN THE RED SEA REGION

The Red Sea region is a complex and diverse area, characterized by a multitude of ethnic and religious groups, each with their own unique histories, cultures, and identities. This diversity, while enriching, has often led to various complications, exacerbating the challenges faced in the region. Ethnic and religious divides have historically played a significant role in shaping political landscapes, fueling conflicts, and hindering efforts for peace and stability.

Ethnic divides in the Red Sea region can be traced back to the colonial era, when European powers, such as Britain, France, Italy, and the Ottoman Empire, exerted control and influence over territories that would later become countries in the region. These colonial powers often favored one ethnic group over another, leading to systemic discrimination and marginalization. The remnants of these historical divisions continue to shape the dynamics of the region today.

In Sudan, the most significant ethnic divide lies between the Arab-dominated government and the marginalized African populations in regions such as Darfur, Blue Nile, and South Kordofan. This divide can be traced back to the British colonial period, during which the Arab elites were favored and given preferential treatment, leading to feelings of resentment and exclusion among non-Arab communities. The long-standing conflicts in these regions, rooted in historical grievances, resource control, and political exclusion, have caused immense suffering and displacement for the affected communities.

Similarly, Eritrea, a country with a complex ethnic makeup, has faced significant challenges due to ethnic divisions. The Tigrinya, Tigre, and Saho communities, among others, have experienced tensions and often felt marginalized by the dominant Tigrigna ethnic group. Colonial legacies, along with socio-economic disparities and limited opportunities, have perpetuated these divisions, leading to political instability, human rights abuses, and widespread emigration from the country.

Djibouti, situated at the crossroads of Africa, the Arabian Peninsula, and the Horn of Africa, has a diverse population consisting of the Issa and Afar ethnic groups, among others. The tensions between these two communities have often erupted into violence, posing a threat to the country's stability. These ethnic divisions in Djibouti can partly be attributed to the colonial legacy of favoring certain ethnic groups for administrative and economic purposes. Over time, this has created a sense of competition and animosity between communities.

Religious divides add another layer of complexity to the region. The Red Sea region is home to a mix of religious groups, including predominantly Muslim populations, along with significant Christian and Jewish communities. Religious differences have often been exploited by rival factions seeking power and control. This has resulted in communal violence, persecution, and discrimination, further deepening the divisions in the region.

In Yemen, religious and sectarian divisions have played a central role in the ongoing civil war. The Houthi rebels, who belong to the Zaidi sect of Shia Islam, have clashed with the Sunni-majority government forces, triggering a devastating conflict. The involvement of regional powers, such as Saudi Arabia and Iran, has further fueled these divisions, turning the conflict into a proxy war and exacerbating the suffering of the Yemeni population.

The intersection of ethnic and religious divides adds complexity to the region's challenges. In Sudan and Eritrea, for instance, some ethnic groups are predominantly Muslim, while others adhere to Christianity or indigenous beliefs. In Sudan, the animosity between the Muslim Arab community and the predominantly Christian African South was a significant factor in the country's two-decade-long civil war that ultimately led to South Sudan's secession. These divisions continue to impact the region's political dynamics and exacerbate tensions between communities.

Ethnic and religious divides complicate efforts for conflict resolution and peace negotiations. When communities are deeply divided along these lines, it becomes challenging for different groups to come together and find common ground. Deep-seated grievances, historical animosity, and distrust can hinder any attempts at reconciliation and hinder the overall stability of the region.

Moreover, the exploitation of ethnic and religious fault lines by outside forces further perpetuates divisions. Some global powers have used these divides to further their geopolitical interests, taking sides and providing support to factions that align with their objectives. This interference only deepens the divisions and prolongs conflicts, making it increasingly difficult to achieve lasting peace and stability.

To address the complications arising from ethnic and religious divides in the Red Sea region, a comprehensive approach is required. This approach should prioritize dialogue, inclusion, and efforts to bridge communal divides. Building trust among ethnic and religious groups and fostering a sense of shared identity can help in reducing tensions and promoting peace.

Additionally, regional and international actors need to recognize the importance of addressing the root causes of these divisions. Socioeconomic development, political inclusivity, and efforts to promote cultural and religious tolerance are essential in creating an environment where ethnic and religious differences are respected and celebrated rather than exploited for political gain.

Efforts towards conflict prevention and resolution

should also include addressing historical grievances, providing equitable access to resources, and ensuring the participation of all communities in governance. Education and awareness programs can play a crucial role in promoting tolerance and understanding. By empowering individuals with knowledge and providing platforms for open dialogue, we can foster a more inclusive and harmonious society.

In conclusion, the ethnic and religious divides in the Red Sea region pose significant challenges to peace, stability, and development. The historical, socioeconomic, and political factors that have contributed to these divisions must be addressed through holistic approaches that prioritize dialogue, inclusivity, and respect for diversity. Only through sustained efforts and genuine commitment can the Red Sea region overcome these complications and build a future characterized by unity, understanding, and prosperity.

B. IMPACT OF SECTARIAN STRIFE ON DIPLOMATIC ATTEMPTS TO RESOLVE THE CRISIS

The impact of sectarian strife on diplomatic attempts to resolve the long-standing crisis in the Red Sea region is not only significant but pervasive, casting a dark and enduring shadow over prospects for peace and stability. Throughout the region, religious and ethnic divisions have become deeply embedded, exacerbating an already intricate and precarious geopolitical landscape.

At the heart of the deep-rooted sectarian strife in the Red Sea region lies the ancient and profound Sunni-Shia divide, originating from a theological and historical disagreement within Islam. This divide has endured for centuries and continues to shape the political, social, and cultural dynamics of the region. The differing interpretations of religious texts and the historical schism between these two branches of Islam have contributed to an environment where religious identities often take precedence over other factors, fueling conflicts and creating a cycle of violence and retaliation.

One of the most prominent manifestations of sectarian strife in the Red Sea region is the ongoing rivalry between Saudi Arabia and Iran, the two regional powerhouses representing the Sunni and Shia branches of Islam, respectively. This rivalry, which is fueled by religious ideologies as well as geopolitical interests, has profound consequences for the region. Saudi Arabia, a predominantly Sunni country, considers itself as the guardian of Sunni Islam and has sought to counter Iran's growing influence, particularly in countries with significant Shia populations such as Iraq, Bahrain, and Yemen. The competition for supremacy between these two regional powers further intensifies religious divisions and exacerbates existing conflicts.

Sectarian divisions have not only become entrenched in the political realm but have also permeated various aspects of society in the Red Sea region. Religious ideologies shape education, media, and social narratives, deepening the divides and fostering a climate of suspicion and animosity towards those from different sects. These divisions often result in discrimination, marginalization, and even violence against individuals or communities deemed as belonging to the "other" sect.

Moreover, within the complex conflicts raging across the Red Sea region, religious identities serve as powerful rallying points, further exacerbating sectarian divisions and perpetuating cycles of violence. Extremist groups, such as the Islamic State (IS) and Al-Qaeda affiliates, exploit these divisions to recruit members and advance their radical ideologies. These groups not only perpetuate violence but also aim to create sectarian fault lines, deepening existing divisions and destroying any prospects for peace and reconciliation.

The pervasive nature of sectarian strife poses a daunting challenge for diplomatic efforts to resolve the crisis in the Red Sea region. Finding a peaceful solution becomes an intricate puzzle due to the complexity of the religious and ethnic divisions. Negotiations are hindered by deep-seated religious animosities and the lack of trust between different sects and their respective supporters. Establishing a common ground that can bridge these divides and build lasting peace requires a comprehensive and nuanced understanding of the religious and historical factors at play.

Furthermore, it is essential to acknowledge that religious factions within the region have become deeply intertwined with extremist ideologies. These extremist groups exploit sectarian divisions to promote their own radical agendas, rejecting any possibility of peaceful resolution or coexistence. Their influence undermines the stability of the region and poses a significant challenge to diplomatic initiatives aimed at ending the crisis.

The sectarian strife prevalent in the Red Sea region also significantly shapes the regional power dynamics. Countries like Saudi Arabia and Iran use their respective religious affiliations and influence over religious communities to build alliances and garner support, further entangling religion with political rivalries. This exploitation of sectarian divisions serves the interests of these powerful actors but perpetuates the cycle of conflict and instability within the region.

The profound impact of sectarian strife on diplomatic efforts further extends to the willingness of different actors to engage in negotiations. Deep-seated religious and ethnic identities can result in mistrust and a fear of marginalization, leading to polarization and the exclusion of certain groups from peace talks. Overcoming this challenge necessitates not only acknowledging the complex religious dynamics but also fostering dialogue, inclusivity, and equal participation among all stakeholders.

To overcome the challenges posed by sectarian strife,

it is imperative to foster dialogue and build trust among different religious and ethnic communities. Addressing the root causes of sectarian divisions through comprehensive social and educational reforms can create an environment that fosters inclusivity, understanding, and tolerance. Furthermore, it is crucial for regional and international actors to prioritize de-escalation and conflict resolution efforts, engaging in sustained and comprehensive diplomacy that acknowledges and seeks to mitigate religious divisions.

In conclusion, the impact of sectarian strife on diplomatic attempts to resolve the crisis in the Red Sea region is far-reaching and deeply entrenched. The historical Sunni-Shia divide, proxy wars driven by religious identification, extremist ideologies, and competing regional power dynamics all contribute to the complexity of finding a peaceful solution. Only through a multifaceted approach that includes building trust among diverse communities, addressing root causes, and promoting comprehensive diplomacy can meaningful progress be made towards resolving the crisis and bringing long-lasting stability to the Red Sea region.

C. THE ROLE OF OUTSIDE FORCES FORMING ALLIANCES BASED ON RELIGIOUS PRINCIPLES

Throughout history, the Red Sea region has been witness to complex dynamics shaped by the influence of outside forces seeking to form alliances based on religious principles. These alliances have far-reaching implications for the geopolitics of the region, exacerbating tensions, and contributing to the perpetuation of conflicts.

One of the most significant examples of religious alliances in the Red Sea region is the rivalry between Saudi Arabia and Iran. These two major regional powers have divergent interpretations of Islam and view themselves as custodians of their respective branches. Saudi Arabia, as the birthplace of Islam and home to the holy cities of Mecca and Medina, sees itself as a leader in the Sunni Muslim world. It has historically sought to exert influence and promote a puritanical form of Sunni Islam known as Wahhabism. This ideology has had far-reaching effects beyond Saudi Arabia, as the country has invested billions of dollars in promoting its interpretation of Islam globally through educational institutions, mosques, and religious outreach programs. The Saudi-Iran rivalry, fueled by religious competition, has led to a proxy war in Yemen, where Saudi Arabia supports the Yemeni government against the Iran-backed Houthi rebels. This conflict has further entangled the Red Sea region in a complex web of religious and geopolitical tensions.

Iran, as the dominant Shiite power in the region, has also cultivated religious alliances to expand its influence.

The 1979 Islamic Revolution in Iran, which overthrew the monarchy and established an Islamic republic, gave rise to a new era of Shiite activism. Iran sought to export its revolutionary ideology to fellow Shiite communities across the Middle East, particularly in Iraq, Lebanon, Syria, and Bahrain. This has led to the formation of Shiite militias, such as Hezbollah in Lebanon and the Popular Mobilization Forces in Iraq, which have played significant roles in regional conflicts. Iran's support for these groups contributes to the deepening sectarian tensions and complicates efforts to resolve the Red Sea crisis.

Religious alliances have not only impacted the rivalry between Saudi Arabia and Iran but have also become a catalyst for the involvement of non-state actors in the Red Sea region. Extremist groups such as al-Qaeda and ISIS have exploited religious ideologies to attract members and engender local support. These groups manipulate sectarian divisions to fuel violence and advance their extremist agendas. Throughout the Red Sea region, from Yemen to Somalia, extremist groups have used a blend of religious rhetoric, social grievances, and political instability to establish footholds and recruit followers.

In Yemen, sectarian fault lines have been exploited by various actors to justify their actions, further entrenching the conflict and deepening religious divisions. The Houthi rebels, representing the Zaidi branch of Shiite Islam, have exploited grievances of marginalization and discrimination to gain support and mobilize their followers. Conversely, forces aligned with the Yemeni government, backed by a coalition led by Saudi Arabia, have framed their fight as a struggle against Iranian influence and the spread of Shia Islam. This sectarian framing of the conflict has fueled a devastating war that has resulted in a humanitarian catastrophe and worsened regional tensions.

In addition to these non-state actors, major global powers have also been drawn into the Red Sea region due to religious considerations. The United States, Saudi Arabia's traditional ally, has cultivated close ties with the kingdom, partly due to shared religious values and strategic interests. The U.S. sees Saudi Arabia as a crucial partner in combating terrorism and maintaining stability in the region. However, this alliance has faced scrutiny due to concerns over human rights violations and the role of Saudi Arabia's religious establishment in promoting extremist ideologies.

Russia, on the other hand, has sought to develop its influence in the Red Sea region by aligning with actors that share its interpretation of Islam, notably those affiliated with Shia Islam. While Russia is not a Muslim-majority country, it has a sizable Muslim population and a historical Muslim presence in regions such as the Caucasus. Russia perceives itself as a defender of traditional religious values and has sought to counterbalance Western influence in the region. Its partnership with Iran and tacit support for the Syrian government in the civil war reflects this endeavor to form alliances based on shared religious and geopolitical interests.

The formation of alliances based on religious principles adds a layer of complexity to the already volatile and multifaceted geopolitical landscape in the Red
Sea region. It deepens divisions between different religious communities, exacerbates existing tensions, and
increases the potential for violence. Furthermore, these
alliances often prioritize short-term gains over long-
term stability, hindering efforts to resolve the Red Sea
crisis and find enduring solutions.

To effectively address the role of religious alliances
in the Red Sea region, it is imperative for diplomatic
efforts to acknowledge and engage with the underlying
religious, ethnic, and sectarian dynamics. Promoting religious tolerance, inclusivity, and interfaith dialogue can
help bridge divides and build trust among different religious communities. International actors must also strive
to mediate conflicts impartially, emphasizing the importance of respecting religious freedoms and protecting
the rights of all individuals, irrespective of their religious
affiliations.

Moreover, it is essential to recognize the multifaceted
nature of these alliances. While religious factors play
a significant role, geopolitical considerations, economic
interests, and historical grievances also contribute to
the formation and shaping of these alliances. By taking
a holistic approach that addresses both the religious
and non-religious dimensions of these alliances, a more
comprehensive understanding of the conflicts in the

Red Sea region can be achieved, thereby enabling the development of more effective and sustainable solutions.

In conclusion, the involvement of outside forces forming alliances based on religious principles has significantly influenced the Red Sea crisis and its ongoing complexity. These alliances exacerbate tensions, perpetuate conflicts, and deepen religious divisions within the region. To foster stability and peaceful coexistence, global actors must acknowledge the impact of religious alliances, promote dialogue, and strive to mediate conflicts in an impartial and inclusive manner. By doing so, the Red Sea region can move closer to resolving the crisis and building a future marked by tolerance, understanding, and sustainable peace.

CONCLUSION

The crisis at the Red Sea continues to pose a serious risk to the stability of international trade, with far-reaching implications for global energy security, geopolitical tensions, and regional conflicts. The recent surge in attacks on commercial ships navigating this critical maritime route that connects the Mediterranean Sea to the Indian Ocean has raised concerns about the vulnerability of the Bab el Mandeb strait and its impact on global supply chains.

The strategic importance of the Bab el Mandeb cannot be understated; it serves as a crucial chokepoint for the transportation of goods and energy resources between Europe, Asia, and Africa. The Red Sea region is responsible for facilitating the movement of a significant portion of global trade, including oil, natural gas, minerals, and manufactured goods. Any disruptions to this vital pathway could lead to severe economic consequences on a global scale.

The effects of the crisis in the Red Sea are already reverberating in the energy markets. The instability in the region has raised concerns about possible interruptions to oil exports, causing a surge in oil prices. Given the heavy reliance on the global market for oil-based economies, such price hikes have significant implications for both producers and consumers. Moreover, the interconnected risks in the nearby Strait of Hormuz, another critical oil shipping route, further escalate concerns about the oil supply chain.

However, the consequences are not limited to the realm of oil. The Red Sea crisis has broader implications for maritime trade and transportation of various commodities. Major shipping companies are facing unprecedented challenges in assessing the risks associated with the Red Sea region and are reconsidering their routes and security protocols. This, in turn, leads to higher operational costs and delays in global supply chains throughout multiple industries.

Behind the crisis in the Red Sea lie complex geopolitical dynamics that exacerbate the situation. The region has long been marred by civil wars, territorial disputes, power vacuums, and proxy conflicts. These conflicts have created a tangled web of influence and interference by major global powers such as the United States, Russia,

Iran, and Saudi Arabia. Their involvement not only complicates potential solutions but also further intensifies the tensions and rivalries within the region.

Moreover, securing control over chokepoints like the Suez Canal and the Bab el Mandeb is of utmost importance to various actors in the Red Sea region and beyond. These chokepoints are not only key to facilitating trade but also hold tremendous strategic value. The ability to control or disrupt these critical waterways grants significant leverage in global politics and influences the balance of power between states and non-state actors.

Interstate rivalry and competition further contribute to the complexities of the Red Sea crisis. Regional powers such as Iran, Saudi Arabia, and Egypt engage in intense rivalries, forming alliances and pursuing their respective geopolitical interests. These rivalries can often spill over into maritime confrontations, threatening the safety and stability of the Red Sea.

The complex dynamics within the Red Sea region are compounded by deeply rooted ethnic and religious divisions. Ethnic groups such as the Houthis in Yemen, the Tigrayans in Ethiopia, and the Beja people in Sudan, as well as religious divisions between Shia and Sunni Muslims, add layers of complexity to the conflict. These divisions have been exploited by both regional and outside forces, leading to the formation of alliances based on religious principles. The resulting intricacies of different alliances and conflicts within the Red Sea region contribute to the complexities and challenges faced in finding a sustainable solution.

Beyond the immediate security concerns, the crisis in the Red Sea region has long-term implications for the social, economic, and humanitarian dimensions. Widespread violence, displacement, and disruption of essential services have exacted a heavy toll on local communities. Impoverishment, food insecurity, and the collapse of basic infrastructure further compound the region's woes, with long-lasting consequences on stability and human development.

Given these complexities, the urgency for immediate global cooperation cannot be overstated. The risks posed by the Red Sea crisis to international trade stability and global energy security demand coordinated action. Diplomatic efforts, increased security measures, and robust collaboration among world leaders, regional powers, and international organizations are crucial for safeguarding the Red Sea and maintaining the smooth operation of global trade.

Failure to address the crisis promptly and effectively could have cascading consequences for the stability of the international system and the well-being of people worldwide. The Red Sea crisis is not isolated; it is intricately intertwined with broader geopolitical dynamics and could potentially exacerbate regional conflicts or fuel the rise of new ones. It is essential to view the crisis holistically and recognize its potential to undermine global peace and prosperity.

The resolution of the Red Sea crisis requires a multi-faceted approach that goes beyond short-term security measures. Strengthening local governance and institutions, promoting inclusive dialogue, and addressing the root causes of the conflicts are crucial steps towards sustainable peace and stability in the region. Collaborative efforts in economic development, social integration, and humanitarian assistance will also be necessary to alleviate the suffering of affected communities and build a foundation for lasting stability.

In conclusion, the crisis in the Red Sea demands a comprehensive long-term solution to ensure stability in the region and global economic well-being. Immediate action and proactive measures are required to safeguard the safety, security, and stability of this critical maritime route. By working together, the international community can navigate the complex challenges presented by the Red Sea crisis and chart a path towards a future that ensures the prosperity and security of all nations.

A. RECAP OF THE SERIOUS RISK THE RED SEA ISSUE POSES TO INTERNATIONAL TRADE STABILITY

The Red Sea issue poses a serious risk to international trade stability, with potential ripple effects that could reach far beyond the immediate region. It not only threatens to disrupt one of the most important maritime routes in the world but also adds to the already complex geopolitical landscape of the Middle East and North Africa.

The historical significance of the Red Sea as a trade route cannot be overstated. For centuries, it has facilitated cultural exchange, trade, and economic growth across nations. Its strategic location as a connection between the Mediterranean Sea and the Indian Ocean has made it a hub for global commerce and a vital lifeline for countries in the region.

However, recent conflicts, development challenges, and geopolitical tensions have turned this vital waterway into a potential hotspot for unrest and instability. One of the primary concerns in this volatile region is the escalating threat of piracy. Pirates, taking advantage of the region's geographical features, political instabilities, and the vulnerability of commercial ships, have executed high-profile attacks, hijackings, and kidnappings. The Bab el Mandeb strait, serving as a gateway to the Red Sea, has become a hotspot for piracy activities. These criminal acts not only endanger the lives of seafarers but also disrupt global commerce and increase insurance costs for shipping companies.

Another key aspect impacting the Red Sea issue is the ongoing conflicts and political rivalries in the Middle East and North Africa. The crisis in Yemen, for example, has significantly affected the stability of the Red Sea region. The Houthi rebels, supported by Iran, have targeted ships passing through the Bab el Mandeb strait, aiming to put pressure on their adversaries. This not only raises security concerns but also escalates tensions between regional powers such as Saudi Arabia, Iran, and their respective allies.

Conflicts in neighboring countries such as Sudan, South Sudan, and Eritrea also spill over into the Red Sea region, further complicating the situation. The border disputes, ethnic tensions, and power struggles in these countries contribute to the overall instability in the region. Additionally, the Red Sea borders countries with a history of civil unrest and fragile governance, such as Somalia and Djibouti, which adds another layer of complexity to the challenges at hand.

Moreover, the Red Sea issue intertwines with the broader struggle for power and influence in the Middle East. Competing geopolitical aspirations and rivalries fuel the instability in the region, as various actors seek to secure their interests through military interventions, proxy wars, and strategic alliances. The Saudi-Iran rivalry, often referred to as a "cold war," plays out in the Red Sea, further complicating efforts to find peaceful resolutions.

Furthermore, religious and sectarian divisions exacerbate the challenges. The Red Sea region encompasses countries with diverse cultural and religious demographics, including Sunni and Shia Muslims, Christians, and various ethnic groups. These differences often form the basis for social and political tensions, adding complexity to the search for stability and cooperation. The involvement of non-state actors, terrorist organizations, and radical ideologies further agitate the already volatile situation.

The consequences of the Red Sea issue extend beyond regional implications. Global energy supply chains are heavily reliant on the stability of this critical trade route. Any disruptions or threats to the flow of oil and gas from the Gulf countries through the Red Sea could lead to a disruption in global energy markets and result in increased prices and economic uncertainty worldwide. This vulnerability highlights the need for robust security measures and international cooperation to safeguard the stability of this crucial trade route.

Moreover, the importance of the Red Sea goes beyond energy resources. It serves as a significant artery for global trade, connecting Asia, Europe, and Africa. Many countries rely on the Red Sea route for the transportation of goods, including vital commodities, raw materials, and manufactured products. Disruptions in this trade route would have severe consequences for supply chains, causing delays, increased costs, and potentially affecting industries and consumers around the globe.

To address these challenges and restore stability in the Red Sea region, a comprehensive approach is required. Regional cooperation, supported by the international community, should focus on addressing the root causes of instability, such as political conflicts, economic grievances, and social divisions. Enhanced maritime security measures, including coordination between naval forces, intelligence sharing, and the deployment of anti-piracy operations, are vital in protecting commercial ships while deterring piracy activities.

Furthermore, diplomatic efforts should be prioritized to de-escalate regional tensions and facilitate dialogue among warring parties. Promoting confidence-building measures, fostering cooperation, and addressing grievances through peaceful means can contribute to long-term stability in the Red Sea region.

The potential of the Red Sea as a catalyst for economic development and regional integration should not be overlooked. The countries surrounding the Red Sea possess immense natural resources, including oil, gas, and minerals. Collaborative efforts to harness these resources sustainably and cooperatively can foster economic growth, create job opportunities, and improve living standards for the local population. Additionally, investments in infrastructure development, such as ports, transportation networks, and logistics systems, can further enhance the potential of the Red Sea as a vibrant trade corridor.

In conclusion, the Red Sea issue poses a significant risk to international trade stability and regional security. With piracy, political conflicts, and geopolitical rivalries at play, urgent attention and global cooperation are needed to address the underlying causes and find sustainable solutions. Failure to do so would not only jeopardize the stability of the Red Sea region but also disrupt global commerce, energy supply chains, and the fragile balance of power in the international arena.

B. EMPHASIS ON THE NEED FOR IMME-
DIATE GLOBAL COOPERATION

The Red Sea crisis unfolding in the region is a grave concern that necessitates urgent attention and immediate global cooperation. The alarming increase in attacks on commercial ships and the potential disruptions to vital maritime routes have raised serious security and economic issues, demanding swift action from the international community.

The precarious situation calls for heightened cooperation between nations, particularly those directly involved in the conflicts, to establish effective security measures and deter further attacks. Joint naval patrols, intelligence sharing, and coordination of military forces are imperative to safeguard the shipping lanes in the Red Sea. This concerted effort will send a clear message that acts of aggression and piracy will not be tolerated, thus ensuring the safety and security of international trade.

Diplomatic engagement plays an equally crucial role in resolving the underlying regional conflicts that contribute to the instability in the Red Sea. The conflicts in Yemen, Sudan, and Eritrea have intertwining factors and require a multifaceted approach. Mediation and negotiation between the warring parties to find peaceful solutions are essential. International organizations such as the United Nations, the African Union, and the Arab League can facilitate these diplomatic efforts by bringing all parties to the table and promoting dialogue.

In Yemen, the conflict between the Houthi rebels and the internationally recognized government has escalated tensions and led to a humanitarian crisis of alarming proportions. The Saudi-led coalition's military intervention has further complicated the situation, with civilian casualties and infrastructure damage adding to the suffering of the Yemeni people. It is imperative that all parties engage in inclusive talks to find a political solution that addresses the root causes of the conflict and ensures the well-being of the Yemeni population.

Sudan, on the other hand, has faced internal conflicts and significant governance challenges over the years. The recent political transition following the ousting of long-time leader Omar al-Bashir has offered a flicker of hope for stability. However, the country continues to grapple with ethnic tensions, rebel movements, and the humanitarian fallout from its conflicts. It is crucial for the international community to support Sudan in its endeavors to establish peace, strengthen governance, and alleviate the suffering of its people.

Eritrea, a nation located on the Red Sea coast, has witnessed its share of internal and external conflicts. The strained relationship with its neighboring countries, particularly Ethiopia, has contributed to regional instability. The lifting of sanctions in 2018 brought an opportunity for Eritrea to re-engage in diplomatic dialogue and seek peaceful resolutions to its outstanding disputes. Encouraging continued diplomacy and cooperation is key to ensuring the long-term stability of the Red Sea region.

In addition to security and diplomacy, economic cooperation is vital to mitigate the adverse effects of the Red Sea crisis on global trade. Over 10% of global trade passes through the Red Sea, making it a crucial artery for international commerce. Collaborative efforts should focus on diversifying supply chains and exploring alternative shipping routes to reduce dependence on the affected region. Investing in port infrastructure and enhancing the capacity of other maritime routes can ensure the continuity of trade in the face of potential disruptions. This requires a comprehensive approach involving governments, international financial institutions, and private sector stakeholders.

Furthermore, the affected countries in the Red Sea region require substantial aid and support to rebuild their economies and infrastructure. The conflict has inflicted extensive damage on critical industries such as agriculture, fisheries, and tourism, exacerbating the humanitarian crisis. International organizations and donor countries must enhance their efforts to provide financial resources, technical expertise, and humanitarian assistance to support the affected populations. By addressing the socio-economic challenges faced by these countries, stability can be restored, fostering an environment conducive to resolving the conflicts.

A robust knowledge-sharing framework is paramount to gaining a deeper understanding of the complex dynamics of the Red Sea region. Research and intelligence-sharing initiatives should be prioritized to identify the underlying causes of the conflicts and formulate effective strategies to address them. Collaborative research projects between academic institutions, joint task forces convened by international organizations, and information-sharing networks can contribute to gathering and analyzing data, enabling policymakers and decision-makers to make well-informed choices.

Moreover, supporting grassroots initiatives and local community engagement is crucial in building long-term stability in the region. Empowering civil society organizations and investing in education and development programs will not only address the immediate consequences of the conflicts but also foster a culture of peace, tolerance, and understanding. By involving local actors in the peace-building process, sustainable solutions can be achieved, bringing about lasting peace and prosperity.

In conclusion, the crisis in the Red Sea region necessitates immediate global cooperation. The safety and security of shipping lanes, the resolution of conflicts through diplomacy, economic stability, and knowledge sharing all demand international collaboration. Only through strong and concerted efforts can the Red Sea crisis be effectively resolved, ensuring stability in the region and safeguarding the global economy. The urgency of the matter underscores the need for swift and decisive actions from the international community to address the challenges and forge a path towards a more secure and prosperous future for the Red Sea region.

C. CALL FOR A LONG-TERM SOLUTION TO ENSURE STABILITY IN THE RED SEA REGION AND THE GLOBAL ECONOMY

The recent increase in attacks and tensions in the Red Sea region highlights the urgent need for a long-term solution to ensure stability. The Red Sea is not only a vital maritime route linking the Mediterranean Sea to the Indian Ocean but also a crucial pathway for global trade, particularly for oil and other commodities.

To that end, international cooperation is imperative. Regional powers, such as Egypt, Saudi Arabia, and Iran, must set aside their differences and work towards a comprehensive resolution of the underlying conflicts that fuel the crisis in the Red Sea. Diplomatic efforts should be undertaken to address territorial disputes, proxy wars, and power vacuums that have contributed to the instability in the region.

One key aspect of achieving stability in the Red Sea

is enhancing maritime security. The Red Sea sees a significant amount of piracy, smuggling, and terrorist activities, making it essential to coordinate and cooperate between regional navies, as well as international powers. Joint naval patrols, intelligence sharing, and capacity-building initiatives should be implemented to ensure the safety and security of maritime traffic. These efforts can be bolstered through the establishment of a dedicated multinational task force, where countries can contribute personnel, equipment, and expertise to combat threats effectively.

Furthermore, efforts should be made to address the socioeconomic issues underlying the instability in the Red Sea region. Poverty, unemployment, and lack of economic opportunities breed unrest and exacerbate existing tensions. Investing in development programs, job creation, and infrastructure projects can help uplift local communities, reduce grievances, and promote stability.

The Red Sea region possesses enormous potential for economic growth due to its strategic location and abundant resources. Investing in sustainable industries, such as renewable energy, fishing, and tourism, can foster economic diversification and reduce dependency on traditional sectors like oil. Promoting regional trade agreements and cross-border economic partnerships can also facilitate economic integration and enhance cooperation among countries in the Red Sea region. Moreover, international financial institutions, such as the World Bank and regional development banks, should provide support and funding for these initiatives, ensuring sustainable economic growth and inclusive development.

In addition to addressing economic issues, environmental protection is crucial in the Red Sea region. The Red Sea is home to rich biodiversity, including coral reefs, marine fauna, and unique ecosystems. However, ongoing conflicts, pollution, and overfishing pose significant threats to these fragile ecosystems. International collaboration should focus on promoting sustainable fishing practices, implementing environmental regulations, and preventing pollution to preserve the Red Sea's ecological integrity. Initiatives can include the establishment of marine protected areas, research programs, and cooperation frameworks that promote sustainable resource management and conservation.

Lastly, it is crucial to engage all relevant stakeholders in finding a long-term solution. International organizations, such as the United Nations, should play a central role in facilitating dialogues and negotiation processes. Engaging local communities, civil society organizations, and academia can provide valuable insights and perspectives, ensuring a comprehensive and inclusive approach towards finding lasting stability. Moreover, cultural and religious diversity in the Red Sea region should be respected and celebrated, as it can serve as a foundation for promoting understanding, tolerance, and peaceful coexistence.

The global economy is heavily reliant on the uninterrupted flow of goods and energy through the Red Sea region. Therefore, the instability and conflicts in this region pose a significant risk to the global economy. It is not only the responsibility of regional powers but also that of major global players, such as the United States, Russia, China, and European countries, to contribute to finding a lasting solution. These stakeholders should prioritize dialogue, mediation, and diplomatic channels to de-escalate tensions, encourage cooperation, and promote shared interests.

As the Red Sea region continues to face numerous challenges, collaboration through platforms like the Red Sea Forum, which aims to promote dialogue and co-operation among regional actors, becomes increasingly important. Such platforms can facilitate the exchange of ideas, development of confidence-building measures, and identification of shared interests, fostering a conducive environment for long-term stability and prosperity.

In conclusion, addressing the crisis in the Red Sea region requires a holistic and long-term approach. Through international cooperation, enhanced maritime security, socioeconomic development, environmental protection, and inclusive dialogue, stability can be achieved. The stakes are high, as the Red Sea crisis impacts not only regional security but also the global economy. It is time for all stakeholders to come together, transcend political differences, and work towards sustaining stability in the Red Sea region, protecting its unique ecosystem, and safeguarding the smooth functioning of international trade.

REFERENCES FOR FURTHER
READING AND RESEARCH

THE ROLE OF MARITIME TRADE IN RED SEA SECURITY

The Red Sea, with its strategic location and historical importance, has long been a vital conduit for global maritime trade. Its significance resides in its connection between the Indian Ocean to the east and the Mediterranean Sea to the north. This positioning makes it a crucial route for international shipping, particularly for goods traveling between Europe, Asia, and Africa. Consequently, ensuring the security of the Red Sea is of paramount importance to both regional and global actors.

1. *Historical Trade Routes:* The Red Sea has been a trading hub for thousands of years, dating back to ancient civilizations such as the Egyptians and the Phoenicians. Historical trade routes, such as the Incense Route and the frankincense trade, have facilitated the exchange of goods, ideas, and cultures across the region. These routes brought wealth and prosperity to cities along the Red Sea coast, such as Jeddah, Aden, and Massawa. The Incense Route, also known as the Spice Route, was a crucial trade network that connected the Arabian Peninsula with the Mediterranean region, including Egypt, Greece, and Rome. This route was primarily used for trading precious spices, including frankincense

and myrrh, which were highly sought after for religious ceremonies, medicinal purposes, and perfumes. The trade of these aromatic resins fueled the economy of ancient kingdoms such as Saba, located in present-day Yemen.

2. *Modern Commercial Shipping:* Today, the Red Sea remains a vital maritime trade route, handling a significant portion of global shipping. The Suez Canal, connecting the Red Sea and the Mediterranean Sea, is one of the world's most crucial chokepoints. It enables vessels to bypass the long and treacherous journey around the African continent, significantly reducing travel time and costs. More than 18,000 ships pass through the Suez Canal annually, with a substantial amount of goods, including oil, natural gas, and manufactured products, being transported. The Suez Canal, inaugurated in 1869, revolutionized global trade by providing a direct passage between Europe and Asia. Prior to its construction, ships had to navigate the perilous Cape of Good Hope, increasing travel times and subjecting vessels to harsh weather and pirate-infested waters. With the opening of the Suez Canal, maritime trade flourished, leading to increased economic interdependence between continents.

3. *Economic Implications:* The stability and security of the Red Sea directly impact the global economy. Any disruption to maritime trade in this region can have severe consequences. For example, attacks on commercial vessels by pirates in the waters off Somalia and Yemen have led to increased costs, insurance premiums, and rerouting of ships, negatively affecting international trade. Furthermore, conflicts and political instability along the Red Sea coast, such as the ongoing civil war in Yemen, can disrupt vital shipping lanes and impede the flow of goods. The Horn of Africa, specifically the waters off Somalia, has been a hotbed of piracy in recent years. Piracy incidents reached their peak in 2011, with numerous vessels being hijacked and crew members held hostage for ransom. These pirate

attacks had a significant impact on global trade, particularly for countries dependent on the Red Sea route. The international community, in collaboration with regional partners, embarked on counter-piracy efforts, such as naval patrols, increased security measures, and international legal frameworks to combat and deter piracy.

4. *Maritime Security Challenges:* The Red Sea faces various maritime security challenges, requiring robust cooperation among regional and international actors. These challenges include piracy, smuggling, illegal fishing, maritime terrorism, and the proliferation of arms. Pirates, particularly in the Gulf of Aden, have targeted commercial ships, holding them for ransom and posing a threat to seafarers and the global shipping industry. Smuggling of arms and illicit goods, including drugs, poses security risks and contributes to regional instability. Illegal, unreported, and unregulated (IUU) fishing is also a significant concern in the Red Sea. Overfishing, often fueled by foreign vessels, depletes fish stocks, disrupts marine ecosystems, and negatively impacts the livelihoods of coastal communities dependent on fishing. IUU fishing not only compromises food security but also undermines efforts to maintain sustainable fishing practices and marine conservation.

5. *Humanitarian Consequences:* The security situation in the Red Sea has also led to significant humanitarian consequences. Ongoing conflicts and violence have resulted in the displacement of populations, widespread hunger, and the disruption of access to basic necessities such as food, water, and medical aid. Yemen, in particular, has experienced a severe humanitarian crisis, with millions of people in need of assistance. Ensuring the security of the Red Sea is not only critical for trade but also for addressing the humanitarian challenges that arise from regional conflicts. The conflict in Yemen, which escalated in 2015, has led to one of the world's most dire humanitarian crises. The protracted conflict, coupled with the blockades

and restrictions on port access, has severely limited the flow of vital aid and humanitarian assistance. The international community, humanitarian agencies, and regional actors have been working to address the urgent needs of the affected population. Ensuring the security of the Red Sea is closely tied to facilitating humanitarian access and supporting efforts to alleviate suffering.

6. *Regional and International Efforts:* To address these maritime security challenges, regional and international efforts have been undertaken. The Combined Task Force 151, led by the United States and other partner nations, has actively conducted counter-piracy operations in the Red Sea and the Gulf of Aden. The European Union Naval Force (EU NAVFOR) has also deployed naval assets to deter and prevent piracy off the coast of Somalia. Additionally, regional actors, such as the Gulf Cooperation Council (GCC) and the Arab League, have collaborated to enhance maritime security measures, including information sharing, capacity building, and joint exercises. The Djibouti Code of Conduct, initiated in 2009, represents a significant regional effort to address maritime security challenges in the Red Sea and the Gulf of Aden. This agreement, signed by 21 countries, aims to promote cooperation, information sharing, and capacity building to combat piracy and other illicit activities. Additionally, international organizations such as the International Maritime Organization (IMO) and the United Nations Office on Drugs and Crime (UNODC) play vital roles in supporting regional efforts and providing technical assistance to enhance maritime security capacities.

7. *Environmental Concerns:* The security of the Red Sea also extends to environmental considerations. The Red Sea is home to diverse marine ecosystems, including coral reefs, mangroves, and seagrass beds, which face threats from pollution, overfishing, and climate change. Protecting and conserving these ecosystems not only safeguards biodiversity but also ensures the sustainable use of marine resources.

The Red Sea's coral reefs, renowned for their vibrant colors and biodiversity, are under significant stress due to various factors. Climate change-induced warming and acidification pose a threat to coral health, leading to coral bleaching and degradation. Pollution from land-based activities, including untreated sewage and industrial waste, contributes to the deterioration of water quality. Sustainable fishing practices and marine conservation efforts, along with broader environmental initiatives, are crucial for preserving the Red Sea's unique and irreplaceable ecosystems.

Therefore, the security of the Red Sea has far-reaching implications for global maritime trade, regional stability, humanitarian concerns, and environmental conservation. Addressing the challenges facedby the Red Sea requires a multifaceted approach that involves the collaboration of regional and international actors. Enhancing maritime security measures, such as naval patrols, information sharing, and capacity building, is crucial to deter piracy, smuggling, and other illicit activities. Counter-terrorism efforts should also be prioritized, as the Red Sea region has been susceptible to maritime terrorism threats.

Furthermore, addressing the root causes of conflicts and political instability in the region is essential for ensuring long-term security. This includes facilitating dialogue, promoting conflict resolution, and supporting efforts to build stable and inclusive governance structures. Such actions can contribute to a more secure and stable Red Sea region, reducing the risks associated with maritime trade.

Humanitarian assistance should be prioritized to address the dire needs of affected populations in conflict-affected countries such as Yemen. Ensuring unfettered access to ports and facilitating the delivery of aid can help alleviate the suffering and address the underlying humanitarian crisis.

Environmental conservation efforts must also be incorporated into the broader security framework. Protecting and preserving the Red Sea's unique marine ecosystems, including coral reefs

and mangroves, is vital for sustaining biodiversity and supporting the livelihoods of coastal communities. Collaborative
actions, such as implementing sustainable fishing practices, reducing pollution, and mitigating the impacts of climate change,
are essential for safeguarding the environmental integrity of
the Red Sea.

In conclusion, the Red Sea's role in maritime trade necessitates a comprehensive approach to address security challenges.
Regional and international cooperation, coupled with efforts to
address root causes of conflicts and promote sustainable development, can contribute to a more secure, prosperous, and
environmentally sustainable Red Sea region. By ensuring the
security of this vital waterway, the international community can
enhance global trade, promote regional stability, alleviate humanitarian crises, and safeguard precious marine ecosystems.

Books, Articles and Online Resources

ROLE OF MARITIME TRADE IN RED SEA SECURITY

The following bibliographic list of references should provide
a comprehensive overview on the role of maritime trade in Red
Sea security from the 20th century to recent times. These references span various aspects, including maritime delimitation,
the impact of big data and AI in the maritime industry, U.S.
naval operational history, security competition in the Red Sea
area, and the broader context of maritime history and international maritime trade.

Charney, Jonathan I., et al. *International Maritime
Boundaries*. 6 vols. Dordrecht, The Netherlands: Martinus

Nijhoff, 1993–2011. This multivolume work is a comprehensive reference on maritime delimitation, examining conceptual, methodological, technical, and legal issues.

Johnston, D. M. *The Theory and History of Ocean Boundary-Making*. Montreal: McGill Queen's University Press, 1988. A leading work on maritime delimitation, offering a functionalist and interdisciplinary theory on the issue.

**Kapoor, D. C., and Adam J. Kerr. ** *A Guide to Maritime Boundary Delimitation*. Toronto: Carswell, 1986. This guide combines legal and technical features in the formation of international norms[1].

Rhee, Sang-Myon. "Sea Boundary Delimitation between States Before World War II." *American Journal of International Law* 76.3 (1982): 555–558. A historical perspective on maritime delimitation principles after the Treaty of Versailles.

**Crist, David. ** *Twilight War: The Secret History of America's Thirty-Year Conflict with Iran*. New York: Penguin, 2013. Provides insights into the U.S. Navy's security roles in the Red Sea region.

Hattendorf, John B., ed. *Oxford Encyclopedia of Maritime History*. Oxford, 2007. A four-volume encyclopedia offering a broad overview of maritime history, including maritime trade[5].

United Nations Conference on Trade and Development (UNCTAD). *Review of Maritime Transport 2021*. This annual review provides an analysis of international maritime trade and port traffic, with implications for Red Sea security. https://unctad.org/system/files/official-document/rmt2021_en_0.pdf

International Maritime Organization (IMO). *Red Sea area*. This resource offers current insights into maritime security and environmental concerns in the Red Sea area. https://www.imo.org/en/MediaCentre/HotTopics/Pages/Red-Sea.aspx

Security competition in the Red Sea area. An analysis by the International Institute for Strategic Studies (IISS) on the evolving security dynamics in the Red Sea region.
https://www.iiss.org/en/online-analysis/online-analysis/2022/11/security-competition-in-the-red-sea-area/

** Meland, Per Håkon & Bernsmed, Karin & Wille, Egil & Rødseth, Ørnulf & Nesheim, Dag Atle. (2021). A Retrospective Analysis of Maritime Cyber Security Incidents. TransNav, the International Journal on Marine Navigation and Safety of Sea Transportation. 15. 519-530. 10.12716/1001.15.03.04. **. This paper discusses cyber security in the maritime industry, highlighting vulnerabilities and previous cyber-attacks that could impact Red Sea security. https://www.researchgate.net/publication/354657671_A_Retrospective_Analysis_of_Maritime_Cyber_Security_Incidents

These references collectively provide a multidisciplinary view of the role of maritime trade in Red Sea security, covering historical, legal, technological, and operational perspectives.

THE SITUATION IN THE RED SEA

Given the complexity of the situation in the Red Sea and the various factors contributing to the instability of maritime trade in the region, including the Israeli war in Gaza, geopolitical tensions, piracy, and regional conflicts, here is a list of scholarly references that can provide a deeper understanding of the subject.

International Chamber of Shipping. "International Chamber of Shipping Statement on the Recent Attacks Against Commercial Ships Transiting the Southern Red Sea and the Gulf of Aden." Accessed February 27, 2024. https://www.ics-shipping.org/statement/international-chamber-of-shipping-statement-on-the-recent-attacks-against-commercial-ships-transiting-the-southern-red-sea-and-the-gulf-of-aden/.

Hill Dickinson LLP. "Israel-Palestine Conflict: The Effect on the Global Shipping Industry." Accessed February 27, 2024. https://www.hilldickinson.com/insights/articles/israel-palestine-conflict-effect-global-shipping-industry.

Hand, Marcus. "Geopolitics, Trade, and the Red Sea Crisis." Seatrade Maritime News, November 29, 2023. https://www.seatrade-maritime.com/containers/geopolitics-trade-and-red-sea-crisis.

Saul, Jonathan. "Red Sea Attacks on Ships Spark Safety Concerns for Sailors." Reuters, November 29, 2023. https://www.reuters.com/world/middle-east/red-sea-attacks-ships-spark-safety-concerns-sailors-2023-11-29/.

Mitzner, Dennis. "Red Sea Tensions: Impact On Global Trade, Retail, And Manufacturing." Forbes, February 19, 2024. https://www.forbes.com/sites/dennismitzner/2024/02/19/red-sea-tensions-impact-on-global-trade-retail-and-manufacturing/?sh=58d3005f66b8.

"Israel – Hamas War: Impact on Shipping." NorthStandard, 2023. https://north-standard.com/insights/news/israel-hamas-war-impact-on-shipping/.

"US Warns Ships of Evolving Threats After Attacks in Red Sea." The Hill, 2024. https://thehill.com/policy/defense/4330625-us-ships-threats-attacks-red-sea-iran/.

"Israel-Palestine Conflict Set to Create Challenges in Maritime Industry While Trade Continues with Caution." Hellenic Shipping News, 2023. https://www.hellenicshippingnews.com/israel-palestine-conflict-set-to-create-challenges-in-maritime-industry-while-trade-continues-with-caution/.

"Red Sea Attacks: What Trade Experts Have to Say About the Shipping Disruptions." World Economic Forum, February 20, 2024. https://www.weforum.org/agenda/2024/02/red-sea-attacks-trade-experts-houthi-shipping-yemen/.

"Israel-Gaza Conflict: Impact on Shipping." Gard, December 11, 2023. https://www.gard.no/web/articles?documentId=36097505.

"The Complicated Nature of Red Sea Geopolitics." Arab Center Washington DC, 2023. https://arabcenterdc.org/resource/the-complicated-nature-of-red-sea-geopolitics/.

"Yemen's Houthi Rebels Seize Cargo Ship in Red Sea and Call Israeli Vessels 'Legitimate Targets'." The Guardian, November 20, 2023. https://www.theguardian.com/world/2023/nov/20/yemen-houthi-rebels-seize-cargo-ship-galaxy-leader-red-sea-israel.

"Are Houthi Red Sea Attacks Hurting Israel and Disrupting Global Trade?" Al Jazeera, December 20, 2023. https://www.aljazeera.com/news/2023/12/20/are-houthi-red-sea-attacks-hurting-israel-and-disrupting-global-trade.

"Red Sea Crisis Exposes a Weak Point of Global Maritime

Trade." Geopolitical Monitor, 2024. https://www.geopoliti-calmonitor.com/red-sea-crisis-exposes-a-weak-point-of-global-maritime-trade/.

"US Warship and Multiple Commercial Ships Come Under Attack in Red Sea." Euronews, December 3, 2023. https://www.euronews.com/2023/12/03/british-military-reports-explosion-off-the-coast-of-yemen-in-the-key-bab-el-mandeb-strait.

"How Can the Israel-Hamas War Impact Maritime Shipping and Supply Chains in General?" Logistics In-sider, 2023. https://www.logisticsinsider.in/how-can-the-israel-hamas-war-impact-maritime-shipping-and-supply-chains-in-general/?amp=1.

"Impact of Geopolitical Tensions in the Red Sea on Réunion Is-land." RSIS, January 15, 2024. https://www.rsis.edu.sg/rsis-publi-cation/rsis/impact-of-geopolitical-tensions-in-the-red-sea-on-reunion-island/.

"Red Sea Ship Hijacking Delivers a Warning on Supply Chain Risks." Nikkei Asia, 2023. https://asia.nikkei.com/Politics/Israel-Hamas-war/Red-Sea-ship-hijacking-delivers-a-warning-on-supply-chain-risks.

"Israel-Hamas Conflict Impacts Shipping." Port Technol-ogy, 2023. https://www.porttechnology.org/news/israel-hamas-conflict-impacts-shipping/.

"Conflict in the Red Sea Makes Economic Waves." Middle East Council, February 22, 2024. https://mecouncil.org/blog_posts/conflict-in-the-red-sea-makes-economic-waves/.

"Chaotic Scenes in the Red Sea as Israeli-Linked Ships

Are Targeted." Splash247, 2023. https://splash247.com/chaotic-scenes-in-the-red-sea-as-israeli-linked-ships-are-targeted/.

"How the Conflict in Israel Can Impact Maritime Security and Trade." Safety4Sea, 2023. https://safety4sea.com/how-the-conflict-in-israel-can-impact-maritime-security-and-trade/.

"Trading Bases: The Red Sea Tinderbox and the Maritime Economy." European Council on Foreign Relations, 2023. https://ecfr.eu/article/trading-bases-the-red-sea-tinderbox-and-the-maritime-economy/.

These references cover a range of perspectives and analyses on the current situation in the Red Sea, including the impact of the Israeli war in Gaza, the role of piracy, and the broader geopolitical implications for maritime security and trade.

www.ingramcontent.com/pod-product-compliance
Lightning Source LLC
Chambersburg PA
CBHW051723020426
42333CB00014B/1122